Spelling Writing and Reading

7th and 8th Grade

Language Arts Curriculum

Natasha Attard Ph.D

Also by Natasha Attard, Ph.D.

The Spelling Practice Workbook 6th Grade: Guided Activities to Increase your Word Power. Consolidates and Complements Homeschooling of the English Language

The Spelling Practice Workbook 7th Grade: Guided Activities to Increase your Word Power. Consolidates and Complements Homeschooling of the English Language

The Spelling Practice Workbook 8th Grade: Guided Activities to Increase your Word Power. Consolidates and Complements Homeschooling of the English Language

Vocabulary and Spelling Practice 7th Grade: Intensive Practice Workbook and Guided Activities to Increase Your Word Power.

Vocabulary Building 7th Grade Workbook: Guided Activities to Increase your Word Power. Consolidates and Complements Homeschooling of the English Language

Spelling High School Workbook Grades 9-10: Vocabulary and Writing Practice with Interactive Activities.

Printed in the USA

ISBN Paperback: 978-9918-9583-8-2

Table of Contents

Author's Message

**Thank you for purchasing
"Spelling, Writing and Reading 7th and 8th Grade"**

Welcome! In writing this book, my aim was to produce a comprehensive curriculum that integrates spelling, writing, and reading into a cohesive and progressive resource. This book is structured to introduce 7th and 8th graders to the basic mechanics of language, progressing to more advanced lessons on writing and reading as their skills develop.

This book is divided into nine parts, with each part focusing on different essential components of language arts. The first four parts of the book are designed to enhance students' spelling abilities through engaging lessons on phonetics, syllabification, spelling rules, and patterns. Each lesson includes a variety of activities aimed at practicing and reinforcing the concepts learned.

Parts 5 through 8 of the book delve into word study and comprehension within context. In these sections, students engage with affixes (prefixes and suffixes), synonyms and antonyms, Greek and Latin roots, and homophones. Each lesson emphasizes Tier 2 vocabulary, crucial for academic writing, and includes a glossary of definitions. This allows students to concentrate fully on the learning objectives of the specific activities and exercises they are undertaking.

The final part of the book is dedicated to various writing texts—narrative, descriptive, expository, and persuasive. It includes lessons on each writing style, followed by model passages to illustrate the concepts discussed. This section also provides multiple-choice questions designed to familiarize students with the types of questions found in standardized tests such as the digital SAT. Additionally, the lessons include guided templates and structured writing exercises to enhance retention and offer practical writing guidance.

Supplementary resources with printable worksheets are included with this purchase to provide extra practice related to the lessons in the book. These resources can be downloaded directly from my website. To access these resources, please use the password provided on page 261 of this book.

Natasha Attard

How to Use this Book

This book is designed to support students in developing skills in spelling, writing, and reading, offering a structured path through the complexities of language arts for 7th and 8th graders. Below is an overview of how each of the nine parts of the book aids in this educational journey:

Introduction to Language Fundamentals:
Parts 1 and 2 of this book utilize a phonics-based approach to improve literacy skills, focusing on the foundational aspects of both vowel and consonant sounds and their application in spelling rules. By exploring these elements, students are equipped to decode and spell words more effectively, enhancing both their reading fluency and writing accuracy. Each lesson contains a glossary of the spelling words focused on, supporting students in fully grasping the material.

Enhancing Spelling Skills:
Parts 3 and 4 build on the foundational lessons from Parts 1 and 2, applying and reinforcing these concepts through diverse spelling activities. This includes the practice of syllabification and applying vocabulary in context. These sections are designed to integrate spelling practice with actual word usage, offering a comprehensive approach to language study and writing skills development.

In-Depth Word Study:
Parts 5 through 8 explore, in-depth, the various facets of words, with the aim to equip students with the skills necessary to recognize and apply complex vocabulary effectively. These parts cover affixes (prefixes and suffixes), Greek and Latin roots, synonyms and antonyms, homophones and frequently misspelled words. The lessons include tables as visual aids to help clarify concepts and improve retention.

Writing and Reading:
Part 9 marks a significant advancement in the students' journey, where they apply the knowledge and skills they've developed to enhance their writing abilities. This section introduces various writing forms that 7th and 8th graders need to master, including narratives, descriptive texts, persuasive essays, expository essays, reports, dialogues, and opinion articles.

Each writing style is illustrated through model texts, which not only guide students through the writing process but also double as reading comprehension exercises. These are followed by multiple-choice questions designed to echo the format of the digital SAT, though less challenging, to prepare students for standardized testing.

Visual aids such as tables help clarify writing concepts, and guided templates are provided to facilitate the students' writing tasks, ensuring they have a structured approach to writing their own texts.

Vocabulary Glossaries

Throughout the book, definitions of Tier 2 academic words introduced in the lessons are provided. Some definitions are included directly within the lessons as required, while other definitions are provided in glossaries at the end of the lessons. For the page numbers of the vocabulary glossaries, please refer to the table of contents.

Common Core State Standards (CCSS)

This book aligns with the following CCSS: CCSS.ELA-LITERACY.L.7.2.B - 8.2.C; CCSS.ELA-LITERACY.RF.7.3.A - 8.3.A; CCSS.ELA-LITERACY.L.7.4.A-8.4.A; CCSS.ELA-LITERACY.L.7.4.B-8.4.B; CCSS.ELA-LITERACY.L.7.5.C-8.5.C; CCSS.ELA-LITERACY.W.7.1-8.1; CCSS.ELA-LITERACY.W.7.2-8.2; CCSS.ELA-LITERACY.W.7.3-8.3; CCSS.ELA-LITERACY.W.7.7-8.7; CCSS.ELA-LITERACY.RL.7.10-8.10.

Answer Key

An answer key is provided for activities where specific answers are needed. Explanations are also included to clarify why certain answers are correct.

Additional Resources Available Online

Additional support is provided through supplementary worksheets, including the answer key, for extra practice. These resources are available on the website https://natashascripts.com. The access information and password are provided on page 261 of this book.

Part 1

Vowel Sounds and Patterns

LESSON 1: Vowel Sounds

Welcome to our first lesson! In this lesson we will practice identifying vowel sounds.

Every "a," "e," "i," "o," and "u" holds the magic of long and short sounds! These vowel sounds are the secret ingredients to pronouncing words just right, mixing and mingling with the rest of the alphabet crew.

Imagine vowels as shape-shifters; with a quick switch of their sound, they can transform "stall" into "still," turn "peck" into "pick," morph "fend" into "find," flip "moss" to "mess," and twist "pole" into "pile." It's like a spelling spell—change the sound, and poof! The word reveals a whole new meaning.

Why study vowel sounds?
In this part of the book, we will practice identifying short and long vowel sounds. Why is this important? A particular vowel sound usually indicates a pattern. It can tell you whether the letter that follows it needs to be doubled or not. For example, the short "o" in "hopping" indicates that the next consonant "p" must be doubled, whereas the long "o" in "hoping" signals that the next consonant "p" must remain single.

Vowel sounds also influence the sounds of the consonants they are connected to. They can make the consonant sound soft or hard. For example, the vowel "e" makes the "c" sound soft, as in "century," but the vowel "o" makes the "c" sound hard as in "cobweb."

Some vowels are silent but they are still hard at work, changing the sound and the meaning of the word. Consider the words "hop" and "hope." Do you notice that the "e" in "hope" changes the sound of the word, turning "o" to a long "o"?

By recognizing sound patterns and how vowels change consonant sounds and word meanings, you'll improve your reading fluency, spelling accuracy, and overall communication skills.

Important Note
You might encounter words whose meanings you're not familiar with—don't worry! These are Tier 2 words, important for academic reading and writing. For now, focus on the vowel sounds. We'll cover their usage in later parts of the book. If you'd like to check the definitions, a list is provided at the end of this part of the book on page 23.

Practice Makes Perfect
We will practice these sounds throughout this part of the book. As we move forward, we'll build on this knowledge to improve your spelling skills, eventually applying these words in various activities.

LESSON 2: The "A" Sounds

The vowel "a" has two basic sounds: long and short. Consider the following "a" sounds:

Long "A"	Short "A"
tape	tap
major	magnet
ancient	alimony

Spotting whether "a" is taking a quick dash or a long leap is key to spelling champions. Identifying the vowel sound in a word will help you **split a long word into smaller easier parts** which will help you learn challenging words more easily and effectively.

major ⟶ ma - jor   magnet ⟶ mag - net
ancient ⟶ an - cient   alimony ⟶ al- i - mo - ny

Activity 1: Read the following words. Do you notice the difference in the "a" sound of each word?

Word Bank 1
Acknowledge
Administer
Amiable
Antagonize
Apprehend
Catalyst
Fallacy
Malady

Word Bank 2
Ache
Acre
Alien
Crave
Debate
Fable
Salient
Wane

1. Word bank _____ has a long "a" sound.

2. Word bank _____ has a short "a" sound.

LESSON 3: The "E" Sounds

The vowel sound "e" has many faces. You've seen it everywhere, from "elephant" to "exercise," but did you know that the "e" has some tricks up its sleeve?

The Short "E" Sound: this sound is quick and to the point, like the "e" in "text" or "flex". Try saying those words out loud and notice how your mouth slightly opens and your tongue stays in the middle, just chilling.

The Long "E" Sound: this sounds just like its name, as in "breeze" or "freeze." Your mouth smiles a bit when you say it, and it feels like the sound is reaching out for something more.

The Sneaky Silent "E": Ever noticed how adding an "e" at the end of some words changes everything? Like "not" turning into "note." That silent "e" doesn't make a sound itself, but it has the power to change the meaning of the word.

The Schwa "E" Sound: this sounds like a quick "uh" in words like "problem." It's the most chill "e" of all, barely there but still making its presence known!

Why do the different "e" sounds matter?
Understanding the "e" helps you spell words correctly and pronounce them like a pro. Plus, it's fun to see how changing one letter can transform a word and its meaning entirely. Let's have a look at some examples.

LESSON 4: The Schwa Sounds

 Did you know that all the vowels (a, e, i, o, u) have a Schwa Sound "uh"? Take a look at these examples.

Schwa "a"

Sof**a**

Agend**a**

About

Schwa "e"

Probl**e**m

Syst**e**m

En**e**my

Schwa "i"

Fam**i**ly

Pet**i**tion

Foss**i**l

Schwa "o"

Mem**o**ry

Econ**o**my

Freed**o**m

Schwa "u"

Alb**u**m

S**u**pply

Walr**u**s

13

Activity 1: Decide which sound each of the underlined letters produces in each word:

	Short	Long	Silent	Schwa "uh"
D<u>e</u>tail	☐	☐	☐	☐
<u>E</u>quilibrium	☐	☐	☐	☐
Probl<u>e</u>m	☐	☐	☐	☐
Facad<u>e</u>	☐	☐	☐	☐
Extr<u>e</u>me	☐	☐	☐	☐
Sev<u>e</u>re	☐	☐	☐	☐
<u>E</u>pidemic	☐	☐	☐	☐
Independ<u>e</u>nt	☐	☐	☐	☐
Enduranc<u>e</u>	☐	☐	☐	☐
Man<u>e</u>uver	☐	☐	☐	☐
En<u>e</u>my	☐	☐	☐	☐
<u>E</u>nvision	☐	☐	☐	☐
It<u>e</u>m	☐	☐	☐	☐
<u>A</u>round	☐	☐	☐	☐
Appreci<u>a</u>te	☐	☐	☐	☐
<u>A</u>stound	☐	☐	☐	☐
C<u>a</u>tastrophe	☐	☐	☐	☐
Deb<u>a</u>te	☐	☐	☐	☐

LESSON 5: The "I" Sounds

Did you know that the "i" is a master of disguise? Like a skilled magician, the "i" has a few sounds up its sleeve!

First there is the long "i" sound which likes to say its own name with pride, as in "precise" and "alibi." Then we encounter the short "i" sound, modest and unassuming, as in "indicate" or "independent."

The "i" has more tricks up its sleeve; it can become inaudible. The silent "i" can be found in words like "business" (pronounced "biz-nis") and "sovereign" (pronounced "sov-rin"). This silent "i" does not perform any real function in the pronunciation of these words but serves to remind us of the words' origins. For instance, the word "business" comes from the Old English word "bisignis," evolving over time to the word we know today. "Sovereign" is derived from the French word "soverain," explaining why the "i" has endured in this word.

Sometimes, the "i" plays a very special role in words, having the power to mimic or influence the sounds of other vowels. For instance, in "machine," the "i" contributes to a long "e" sound, reminiscent of the sound in "seen." The "i" also has the power to transform a sound when it is accompanied by another vowel, such as "raid," "hilarious," and "opinion."

Activity 1: Decide if the "i" sound is long or short.

	L	S		L	S
Invoke	☐	☐	Impede	☐	☐
Implore	☐	☐	Incite	☐	☐
Abide	☐	☐	Inviolable	☐	☐
Defiant	☐	☐	Immense	☐	☐
Quagmire	☐	☐	Infuriate	☐	☐
Filter	☐	☐	Deride	☐	☐

LESSON 6: The "O" Sounds

 The "o" is a multifaceted vowel, much like a gemstone. It shifts and changes like the sea under the moon's pull.

Meet the "o" in "ocean," a long and round open sound which stretches out the moment in words like "odor" and "erosion." It's cousin, the short "o," is more modest. It prefers a quick appearance in words like "<u>o</u>ffspring" and "<u>o</u>bsolete."

When it teams up with other vowels like "oo," "oa," "oe," and "oi," a whole new sound is produced. Notice how this happens: **swoon, coastal, shoelace and connoisseur.**

Let's not forget the silent "o" in words like "colonel" (pronounced *ker-nuhl*) and "leopard" (pronounced "lep-erd"). Here the "o" takes a vow of silence, letting the other letters do the talking.

Activity 1: Decide if the "o" sound is long or short.

	L	S		L	S
Overdue	☐	☐	R**o**bust	☐	☐
Occurrence	☐	☐	Prov**o**ke	☐	☐
Obscure	☐	☐	Er**o**sion	☐	☐
Obsolete	☐	☐	**O**minous	☐	☐
Alim**o**ny	☐	☐	**O**scillate	☐	☐
Forecl**o**sure	☐	☐	Gr**o**tesque	☐	☐

16

LESSON 7: The "U" Sounds

The sounds of the vowel "u" are as varied as the creatures in a bustling jungle! First, we have the short and quick "u" sound, like the one you hear in "cumbersome" and "mutter." It's snappy and doesn't take much time to say. Now, let's meet the sneaky schwa sound in words like "circumstance" and "syllabus," whispering a quiet, quick sound "uh."

Next up, compare the "u" sound in "bushy" and "bulwark." The "u" sound in these words is different from that in "cumbersome" and "syllabus." It's short, but it sounds like the "u" in "put."

Now, let's explore the long and dragging "u" sound in words like "unanimous" and "utilize." This sound feels like it stretches out, like a long, relaxing "yoo."

Finally, consider words like "allude" and "prelude." These words have the long "u" which is similar to the sound in "moon" and "soon," but different from the "yoo" sound in "unanimous."

By comparing these words, you can hear how the "u" sound changes its tune, making each word unique and full of character.

Activity 1: Decide if the "u" sound is long or short.

	L	S		L	S
Fundamental	☐	☐	Rupture	☐	☐
Unique	☐	☐	Refuse	☐	☐
Amuse	☐	☐	Accuse	☐	☐
Succumb	☐	☐	Nurture	☐	☐
Judgment	☐	☐	Consumable	☐	☐
Humane	☐	☐	Plummet	☐	☐

LESSON 8: Words with "ie" and "ei"

 Ready to crack the code of the "i" and "e" mystery? Let's start with this catchy old rhyme:

I before e
<u>except</u> after c
or when sounding like ay
in neighbor and weigh
or when sounding like eye
in seismic and height

This fun little rhyme serves as a handy rule of thumb for spelling words where "ie" and "ei" combine to make a single sound, like in "hygiene" and "receive." But remember, it's all about the sound! If the letters don't blend into one sound—as in "science" and "society"—then this clever rhyme doesn't apply.

Let's simplify this catchy old rhyme. Below, you'll find the rules from the rhyme broken down into easy-to-follow guidelines. Accompanying them is a table that helps you visualize when to use "ie" and "ei" based on the sounds they make. Use this table as your quick reference guide to learn these tricky spelling combinations.

The Rules

#1. When a word has a long "ee" sound, as in "believe," and is NOT followed by the consonant "c," the order of "i" and "e" is "ie."

#2. When the long "ee" sound is followed by a "c," the order changes to "ei."

#3. When a word has a long "ay" sound, as in "neighbor," the order of "i" and "e" is "ei."

#4. When a word has a long "eye" sound, like in "height," the order is also "ei."

Refer to the table below to better visualize these rules from the traditional rhyme.

SOUND	CONSONANT	ORDER	EXAMPLES	EXCEPTIONS
ee	any	**ie**	**die**sel g**rie**f **chie**f a**chie**ve **yie**ld **sie**ge	patient quotient friend
ee	c	**ei**	per**cei**ve **cei**ling de**cei**ve con**cei**ve re**cei**pt de**cei**t	ancient sufficient conscience proficient efficient species
ay	any	**ei**	**nei**ghbor **wei**gh sur**vei**llance s**lei**gh **vei**n **wei**ght **rei**ndeer **ei**ght **rei**n	counterfeit sovereign surfeit
eye	any, but usually following "h"	**ei**	apart**hei**d **hei**ght **hei**st Fahren**hei**t	die lie tie pie

Exceptions

Rule #1 states that if a word has a long "ee" vowel sound, the order should be "ie." However, there are exceptions where a short vowel sound still takes the "ie" order. Let's review the few words that fall into this exception:

> patient   quotient   friend

Rule #2 states that when the long "ee" sound is followed by a "c," the order typically changes to "ei." However, there are exceptions to this rule:

ancient	proficient	glacier
sufficient	efficient	
conscience	omniscient	
deficient	species	

Rule #3 states that if a word has a long "ay" sound, as in "neighbor," the order of "i" and "e" is "ei." However, there are a few words that use the "ei" order without having the "ay" sound, instead having a short "i" sound:

> counterfeit   sovereign   surfeit

Rule #4 states that when a word has a long "eye" sound, as in "height," the order is "ei." However, there are a few words with the "eye" sound that follow the "ie" order instead.

> die   lie   tie   pie

Activity 1: Complete the sentences using the correct word from the word bank, focusing on the placement of "i" and "e." Refer to the definitions at the end of this activity if you need clarification on any words.

Lie	Ancient	Neighbor	Perceive
Counterfeit	Patient	Surveillance	Yield
Sovereign	Heist	Receipt	Achieve
Efficient	Reindeer	Deceive	Grief

1. Despite the harsh weather, the farmer's fields _____ an impressive amount of crops this season.

2. To _____ about one's whereabouts is often considered a breach of trust among friends.

3. The doctor praised her little _____ for showing bravery and calm during the long treatment.

4. The sudden loss of her beloved cat enveloped Clara in a deep _____ that lingered for weeks.

5. Always keep your _____ in case you need to return something you bought.

6. The history class discussed the role of a _____ in medieval times and how kings and queens exercised their powers.

7. The bank installed new _____ cameras to enhance security after the recent robbery.

8. With relentless dedication, Noah was able to _____ his goal of reading fifty books over the summer.

9. The magician's skill to _____ the audience with his clever illusions was unmatched.

10. The movie about the bank _____ had everyone on the edge of their seats with its thrilling plot twists and unexpected betrayals.

21

Lie	Ancient	Neighbor	Perceive
Counterfeit	Patient	Surveillance	Yield
Sovereign	Heist	Receipt	Achieve
Efficient	Reindeer	Deceive	Grief

11. The police warned the public about a surge in _____ money circulating in the area.

12. As she entered the dimly lit room, Leah could barely _____ the shapes of furniture scattered about.

13. Sophia baked cookies to welcome the new _____ who moved in next door.

14. The museum's new exhibit featured artifacts from an _____ civilization that once thrived in South America.

15. To be more _____ with his study time, Jayden developed a schedule that allotted specific hours for each subject.

16. During their trip to Finland, they went on a sleigh ride pulled by a team of _____.

Vocabulary Glossary

A

Abide: To accept or act in accordance with.
Accuse: To charge someone with an offense or crime.
Ache: To feel a continuous or prolonged pain.
Achieve: To successfully reach a desired goal or result.
Acknowledge: To accept or admit the existence or truth of.
Acre: A unit of land area equal to 4,840 square yards.
Administer: To manage or oversee the execution of.
Alien: A foreigner; someone from another country.
Alimony: Financial support given to a spouse after separation or divorce.
Amiable: Having a friendly and pleasant manner.
Amuse: To entertain or cause to laugh.
Ancient: Belonging to the very distant past.
Antagonize: To cause someone to become hostile.
Apartheid: A policy of racial segregation and discrimination.
Appreciate: To recognize the full worth of.
Apprehend: To arrest or take into custody.
Around: On every side or all sides of.
Astound: To shock or greatly surprise.

C

Catalyst: A substance that increases the rate of a chemical reaction without itself undergoing any permanent change.
Catastrophe: A sudden and widespread disaster.
Conceive: To form or devise a plan or idea in the mind.
Connoisseur: An expert judge in matters of taste, especially in fine arts, food and wine.
Consumable: An item that is intended to be used up and replaced.
Counterfeit: Made in exact imitation of something valuable with the intention to deceive or defraud.
Crave: To feel a powerful desire for something.

D

Debate: A formal discussion on a particular topic.
Deceit: The act of deceiving or misleading.
Deceive: To cause someone to believe something that is not true.
Defiant: Showing resistance or disobedience.
Deficient: Lacking in some necessary quality or element.
Deride: To mock or ridicule.
Detail: An individual feature, fact, or item.

E

Efficient: Achieving maximum productivity with minimum wasted effort or expense.
Endurance: The ability to endure an unpleasant or difficult process or situation without giving way.
Enemy: A person who is actively opposed or hostile to someone or something.
Envision: To imagine or picture in the mind.
Epidemic: A widespread occurrence of an infectious disease in a community at a particular time.
Equilibrium: A state of balance.
Erosion: The gradual destruction or diminution of something.
Extreme: Reaching a high or the highest degree; very great.

F

Fable: A short story, typically with animals as characters, conveying a moral.

Fallacy: A mistaken belief, especially one based on unsound argument.

Façade: The front of a building, especially an imposing or decorative one.

Filter: A device or process that removes unwanted material from a substance.

Foreclosure: The process of taking possession of a mortgaged property as a result of the mortgagor's failure to keep up mortgage payments.

Fundamental: Forming a necessary base or core; of central importance.

G

Grotesque: Comically or repulsively ugly or distorted.

H

Heist: A robbery or theft.

Humane: Showing compassion or benevolence.

I

Immense: Extremely large or great, especially in scale or degree.

Impede: To delay or prevent by obstructing.

Implore: To beg earnestly or desperately.

Incite: To encourage or stir up violent or unlawful behavior.

Independent: Free from outside control; not subject to another's authority.

Infuriate: To make someone extremely angry and impatient.

Inviolable: Never to be broken, infringed, or dishonored.

Invoke: To call on a higher power for assistance or as an authority.

Item: An individual article or unit, especially one that is part of a list, collection, or set.

J

Judgment: The ability to make considered decisions or come to sensible conclusions.

M

Magnet: An object that produces a magnetic field and attracts iron or steel.

Major: Important, significant, or greater in scope.

Malady: A disease or ailment.

Maneuver: A movement or series of moves requiring skill and care.

N

Nurture: To care for and encourage the growth or development of.

O

Obscure: Not well known; difficult to understand.

Obsolete: No longer in use; out of date.

Occurrence: An event or incident.

Ominous: Giving the impression that something bad is going to happen.

Omniscient: Knowing everything.

Oscillate: To move or swing back and forth in a regular rhythm.

Overdue: Not done or happening when expected or needed; late.

P

Perceive: To become aware or conscious of something.

Plummet: To fall or drop straight down at high speed.

Problem: A matter or situation regarded as unwelcome or harmful and needing to be dealt with.

Proficient: Competent or skilled in doing or using something.

Provoke: To stimulate or give rise to a reaction or emotion, typically a strong or unwelcome one, in someone.

Q

Quagmire: A complex or hazardous situation; a soft, boggy area of land that gives way underfoot.

Quotient: The result obtained by dividing one quantity by another.

R

Receipt: A written acknowledgment of having received something.

Refuse: To indicate unwillingness to accept or do something.

Robust: Strong and healthy; vigorous.

Rupture: To break or burst suddenly.

S

Salient: Most noticeable or important.

Severe: Very great; intense.

Siege: A military operation where forces surround a place to compel surrender.

Sleigh: A vehicle on runners for conveying goods or passengers over snow or ice.

Sovereign: A supreme ruler, especially a monarch.

Species: A group of living organisms consisting of similar individuals capable of exchanging genes.

Succumb: To fail to resist pressure, temptation, or some other negative force.

Surfeit: An excessive amount of something.

Surveillance: Close observation, especially of a suspected spy or criminal.

Swoon: To faint from extreme emotion.

U

Unique: Being the only one of its kind; unlike anything else.

W

Wane: To decrease in size, extent, or degree.

Y

Yield: To produce or provide; to give way to arguments, demands, or pressure.

Part 2
The Role of Consonants

LESSON 9: Meet the Consonants

 Consonants are like the building blocks of words. They give words their structure and shape. Think of them as the walls and floors of a house—without them, things would be pretty shaky!

There are 21 consonants in the English alphabet, and each one brings its own unique sound. From the hard-hitting "k" in "kite" to the buzzing "z" in "buzz," consonants add spice and strength to our words.

Consonants are not just standalone players; they love to collaborate. When "c" and "h" come together, they create the "ch" sound found in words like "chocolate" and "bunch." Interestingly, this pair can also produce a "k" sound as seen in "chorus" and "chord." It's this versatility that makes studying consonants so intriguing!

Consider the letter "q," a peculiar consonant that almost always pairs with the letter "u" followed by another vowel, forming combinations seen in words like "quaint," "quest," "qualify," "quintessence," and "Albuquerque." This pairing is consistent across various contexts, though there are exceptions like geographical names "Iraq" and "Qatar." However, other place names still follow the usual rule, such as "Quebec," "Quito," and "Frequente."

Just like vowels, consonants can also vary in their pronunciation, exhibiting hard or soft sounds. For instance, the "g" in "gullible" and "glide" shows its harder side, while in "gymnasium" and "manage," it softens. The letter "c" follows a similar pattern, sounding sharp in "camel," "cucumber," and "panic," but softening in "cent" and "precision."

Doubling consonants is another intriguing aspect of English spelling. Words like "abbey," "account," and "cuddle" illustrate how consonants double up following a short vowel sound. This rule also applies when adding suffixes such as "ed" or "ing," as in "beginning" and "grabbed."

Lastly, let's not overlook the silent consonants, those tricky letters that appear in writing but remain unheard in pronunciation. You've already encountered an example in previous lessons with the word "succumb," where the "b" is silent, giving the impression the word ends in "m."

This introduction is just the beginning! As we continue our exploration into the behavior of consonants in words, you'll begin to recognize patterns and rules that illuminate how English words are used and spelled. This deeper understanding will not only improve your grasp of language mechanics but also enhance your spelling skills.

LESSON 10: Using the Same Consonants to Enhance Writing

Let's start by exploring an example of how using words with the same consonants can enrich creative writing. This will help us see the effect that deliberate consonant use has on enhancing the narrative and engaging the reader. Are you ready to dive in and discover the power of consonants in action?

Activity 1: Read the following narrative, observe the words that use the same consonants, and note their effect on the narrative. Then, answer the questions that follow.

The Strange Star of Riverside Town

In the small town of Riverside, something strange stirred under the starlit sky. Every night, the residents could hear a soft rustling, not from the wind-swept trees but something more mysterious. It began when old Mrs. Thompson reported seeing twinkling lights by the river.

Hunter, a curious teenager and an amateur stargazer, decided to investigate. Armed with his flashlight, he tiptoed toward the river to trace the source of the strange twinkling.

As the stars blinked silently above him, Hunter stumbled upon a tiny, trembling starling, its wings wrapped in a shimmer of frost. Realizing it was hurt, he carefully wrapped the bird in his scarf and rushed home.

Hunter took great care of this magical creature and nurtured it back to health. He named it Spark, for its resilience and the tiny sparks of light it seemed to scatter when it first arrived.

As the seasons turned, Spark grew stronger under Hunter's nurturing care. When the starling had fully recovered, Hunter knew it was time to let his feathered friend go to continue exploring the world. As he watched Spark fly away, he thought to himself that a star doesn't need to be in the sky to shine brightly.

Alliteration is when words close together start with the same sound, like "frosty Fridays" or "big blue ball." It makes writing sound catchy and rhythmic.

1. Alliteration and Consonant Use :

In the phrase "something strange stirred under the starlit sky," how does the repetition of the "s" and "str" sounds contribute to the mood of the opening scene?

----

2. Exploring Alliteration:

Find examples of alliteration in the narrative. How does the use of alliteration with consonants such as "s" in "stars silently" and "t" in "tiptoed toward" enhance the mood or imagery?

----

3. Consonant Sounds:

Discuss the impact of the consonant sounds in "tiny, trembling starling." How do these sounds help convey the condition of the starling and add to the tension in the story?

----

4. Repeated Consonant Effects:

What effects does the repeated consonant sound "r" in the phrase "wrapped in his scarf and rushed home" produce in describing Hunter's actions?

----

5. Role of Consonants in Setting:

Consider how the consonant sounds in "soft rustling" and "wind-swept trees" contribute to building the setting. What auditory imagery do these sounds create?

LESSON 11: Hard and Soft Consonants "c" and "g"

 Did you know that the letters "c" and "g" are a bit like chameleons? Depending on their neighbors, they can change their sounds!

When "c" hangs out with "a," "o," or "u,"as in "cat," "cod," and "cute," it sounds hard like a "k." But when it meets "e," "i," or "y," it softens up, sounding like an "s" in "cent," "civic," and "cyst."

The letter "g" follows a similar pattern—it's tough and hard when paired with "a," "o," or "u," as in "game," "gone," and "gut," but goes gentle and soft with "e," "i," or "y," like in "gem," "giraffe," and "gym." Here's a quick list for these rules for your reference:

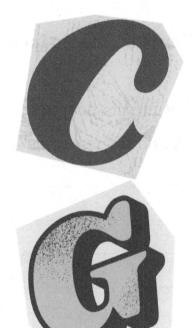

"**C**" is usually

- **hard** before **"a," "o," "u,"** (Cascade, Cohesion, Culminate).

- **soft** before **"e," "i," "y,"** (Cement, Celery, Centrifuge).

Similarly,

"**G**" is usually
- **hard** before **"a," "o," "u,"** (Gallery, Gossip, Guard).

- **soft** before **"e," "i," "y,"** (Gentle, Ginger, Gypsum).

Activity 1: Determine whether the "c" and "g" in each word are pronounced with a soft or hard sound by following the established rules.

Conflict _____   Grapple _____   Census _____

Govern _____   Ceremony _____   Genesis _____

Gesture _____   Cynical _____   Cilantro _____

Germinate _____   Compress _____

Conclude _____

32

LESSON 12: The Silent Consonants "g" and "h"

In the English language, many consonants appear in writing but remain unspoken, like undercover agents. These silent letters reflect the historical changes in pronunciation or come from words borrowed from other languages.

Among the most common silent letters are the "g" and "h," but almost every letter can have a silent role in certain words. Below is a list of words with the silent consonants "g" and "h." Practice spelling these words while keeping in mind the silent consonants, which remain unseen and unheard.

Activity 1: Write the spelling words below twice. Each word features a silent "g." After spelling each word, read its definition. We will be practicing their usage in later parts of this book.

Gnaw   _____   _____

Gnarled   _____   _____

Foreign   _____   _____

Campaign   _____   _____

Design   _____   _____

Impugn   _____   _____

Poignant   _____   _____

Sovereign   _____   _____

Reign   _____   _____

Feign   _____   _____

Align   _____   _____

Definitions

- **Gnaw:** To bite or chew on something repeatedly.
- **Gnarled:** Twisted and rough, especially with age.
- **Foreign:** From, found in, or characteristic of a country or language not your own.
- **Campaign:** A series of planned activities towards a specific goal, often used in politics or marketing.
- **Design:** To plan and make decisions about something that is being built or created.
- **Impugn:** To challenge or question the truth or honesty of something or someone.
- **Poignant:** Evoking a keen sense of sadness or regret.
- **Sovereign:** A ruler or monarch.
- **Reign:** The period during which a sovereign rules.
- **Feign:** To pretend to be affected by a feeling, state, or injury.
- **Align:** To arrange things so that they form a line or are in proper position.

Activity 2: Practice spelling the words listed below, each featuring a silent "h." After spelling each word, read its definition.

Honor   _____   _____

Honest   _____   _____

Exhaust   _____   _____

Heir   _____   _____

Rhythm   _____   _____

Rhetoric   _____   _____

Rhombus   _____   _____

Exhibit   _____   _____

Vehicle   _____   _____

Ghost   _____   _____

Wharf   _____   _____

Definitions

- **Honor:** Respect or recognition given to someone for their honesty or achievements.
- **Honest:** Telling the truth and being fair and trustworthy.
- **Exhaust:** To make someone extremely tired; also refers to the fumes expelled from an engine.
- **Heir:** A person who is legally entitled to receive someone's property, title, or position after they die.
- **Rhythm:** A regular pattern of sounds, words, or actions.
- **Rhetoric:** The skill of using language effectively, especially to persuade or influence people.
- **Rhombus:** A four-sided shape where all sides have equal length but angles are not right angles.
- **Exhibit:** To display or show something publicly in places like museums.
- **Vehicle:** Something used for transporting people or goods, like a car, bus, or bicycle.
- **Ghost:** The spirit of a dead person that some people believe can appear to the living.
- **Wharf:** A platform built on the shore or out from the shore beside which ships can load and unload.

Lesson 13: The Silent "b"

Let's explore words with the silent "b." Typically, these words end with a "b" preceded by an "m," or the "b" couples with a "t" to become silent. We've already encountered the word "succumb" in previous lessons.

Now, let's explore a few more words that follow these patterns. Here's a quick list of the two patterns:

- **Silent "b" after "m"**
  In words like "thumb" and "dumb," the "b" follows an "m" and is not pronounced.

- **Silent "b" with "t"**
  In words like "debt" and "doubt," the "b" couples with a "t" and remains silent.

Activity 1. Review the list of words with the silent "b" and their definitions below. Afterward, proceed to the spelling activity.

Silent "b" after "m"
- **Thumb:** The short, thick first digit of the human hand, set lower and apart from the other four.
- **Limb:** An arm or leg of a person or four-legged animal, or a large branch of a tree.
- **Dumb:** Unable to speak, typically because of congenital deafness.
- **Climb:** Go or come up a (slope or staircase); ascend.
- **Bomb:** An explosive weapon detonated by impact, proximity to an object, a timing mechanism, or other means.
- **Tomb:** A large vault, typically an underground one, for burying the dead.
- **Comb:** A strip of plastic, metal, or wood with a row of narrow teeth, used for untangling or arranging the hair.
- **Womb:** The organ in the lower body of a woman or female mammal where offspring are conceived and in which they gestate before birth.
- **Crumb:** A small fragment of bread, cake, or cracker.
- **Plumb:** Measure (the depth of a body of water).

Silent "b" with "t"
- **Debt:** Money that is owed or due.
- **Doubt:** A feeling of uncertainty or lack of conviction.
- **Subtle:** So delicate or precise as to be difficult to analyze or describe.
- **Subtlety:** The quality or state of being subtle.
- **Subtlest:** Of the highest degree of subtleness.

Silent "b" after "m"

Thumb   _____   _____

Limb   _____   _____

Dumb   _____   _____

Climb   _____   _____

Bomb   _____   _____

Tomb   _____   _____

Comb   _____   _____

Womb   _____   _____

Crumb   _____   _____

Plumb   _____   _____

Silent "b" with "t"

Debt   _____   _____

Doubt   _____   _____

Subtle   _____   _____

Subtlety   _____   _____

Subtlest   _____   _____

Lesson 14: The Silent "c," "l," "n," and "w"

We will now explore the silent letters "c," "l," "n," and "w." These silent letters are less common than the letters we have discussed so far. Read through the rules for each silent letter below and then complete the spelling activities that follow. A list of definitions of words with silent letters is provided at the end of this lesson.

Silent "c"

Rule: The silent "c" often follows an "s" to create a soft sound, though there are a few exceptions where it can appear in other combinations.

Examples: Scent, Ascend, Conscience, Science, Crescent, Muscle, Scissors, Scene.

Exceptions: Indict, Czar, Yacht.

Silent "l"

Rule: The silent "l" is usually found in the middle of a word and followed by a consonant, adding a twist to the pronunciation.

Examples: Salmon, Half, Chalk, Alms, Talk, Should Could, Folk, Yolk, Calf, Psalm, Palm.

Silent "n"

Rule: The silent "n" typically appears at the end of a word, just after an "m."

Examples: Autumn, Column, Hymn, Solemn, Condemn, Damn.

Silent "w"

Rule: The silent "w" generally appears at the beginning of words followed by an "r" and less commonly, by an "h." However, keep an eye on a few exceptions.

Examples ("r"): Wrap, Wrapper, Wrath, Write, Wrong, Wretch, Wrinkle, Wriggle, Wrist, Awry.

Examples ("h"): Who, Whom, Whose, Whole.

Exceptions: Answer, Two, Sword, Yawn.

Activity 1: Review the examples of silent consonants discussed above. Select at least four words from each silent letter category ("c," "l," "n," "w") and write them in the designated columns provided below.

Silent "c"	Silent "l"	Silent "n"	Silent "w"
-----------------	-----------------	-----------------	-----------------
-----------------	-----------------	-----------------	-----------------
-----------------	-----------------	-----------------	-----------------
-----------------	-----------------	-----------------	-----------------
-----------------	-----------------	-----------------	-----------------
-----------------	-----------------	-----------------	-----------------
-----------------	-----------------	-----------------	-----------------
-----------------	-----------------	-----------------	-----------------
-----------------	-----------------	-----------------	-----------------
-----------------	-----------------	-----------------	-----------------

Here are the definitions for silent letter words that you should learn:

Silent "c"
- **Scent:** A distinctive smell.
- **Ascend:** To go up or climb.
- **Conscience:** A person's moral sense of right and wrong.
- **Science:** The study of the natural world based on facts learned through experiments and observation.
- **Crescent:** The curved shape of the visible part of the moon when it is less than half.
- **Muscle:** A band or bundle of fibrous tissue in the body that has the ability to contract, producing movement or maintaining position.
- **Scene:** A place where an incident in real life or fiction occurs or occurred.
- **Indict:** Formally accuse or charge with a serious crime.
- **Czar:** An emperor of Russia before 1917.
- **Yacht:** A medium-sized sailboat or motorboat used for private cruising, racing, or other noncommercial purposes.

Silent "l"
- **Salmon:** A popular edible fish that lives in both fresh and salt water, depending on the stage of its life cycle.
- **Alms:** Money or food given to poor people.
- **Folk:** People in general, or a certain group of people.
- **Yolk:** The yellow internal part of a bird's egg, which is rich in protein and fat.
- **Calf:** A young bovine animal, especially a domestic cow or bull in its first year.
- **Psalm:** A sacred song or hymn, in particular any of those contained in the biblical Book of Psalms. *(Note that the "p" in "psalm" is also silent. We will explore the silent "p" in Lesson 16, on page 41.)*

Silent "n"

- **Solemn:** Not cheerful or smiling.
- **Condemn:** Express complete disapproval of, typically in public; censure.

Silent "w"
- **Wrath:** Extreme anger.
- **Wretch:** An unfortunate or unhappy person.
- **Wriggle:** Twist and turn with quick squirming movements.

Lesson 15: The Silent "k"

Let's explore words with the silent "k." Typically, these words start with a "k" followed by an "n." Review the list of words with the silent "k" and their definitions below. Afterward, proceed to the spelling activity.

- **Knack:** A special skill or ability for doing something quickly or efficiently.
- **Knoll:** A small, rounded hill or mound.
- **Knead:** To work and press dough with the hands to combine and soften it.
- **Knight:** A man granted an honorary title of knighthood by a monarch for military service or other personal merits.
- **Knit:** To make (textiles or garments) by interlocking loops of yarn with needles.
- **Knowledge:** Information, understanding, or skill that you get from experience or education.
- **Knapsack:** A bag carried by a strap on your back or shoulder, often used by hikers.
- **Knave:** A dishonest or unscrupulous man; in card games, another term for the Jack card.
- **Knobble:** To make knobs, lumps, or hard bumps, especially for decoration.
- **Knockout:** An extremely attractive or impressive person or thing; also refers to a method of winning in boxing by incapacitating one's opponent.
- **Knuckle:** The part of a finger at the joints where the bones connect, especially noticeable when the fingers are bent.

Activity 1: Spell and Write.

Knack   _____   _____   _____

Knoll   _____   _____   _____

Knead   _____   _____   _____

Knight   _____   _____   _____

Knit   _____   _____   _____

Knowledge   _____   _____   _____

Knapsack   _____   _____   _____

Knave   _____   _____   _____

Knobble   _____   _____   _____

Knockout   _____   _____   _____

Knuckle   _____   _____   _____

Lesson 16: The Silent "p"

Let's explore words with a silent "p." Did you know that the silent "p" often has Greek origins? Although not all words with a silent "p" come from Greek, many do. In the next activity, start by reading the definitions of the words, then practice writing each word twice.

- **Cupboard:** A cabinet or closet used for storing dishes, food, or other household items.
- **Coup:** A sudden, violent, and illegal seizure of power from a government.
- **Pneumonia:** A lung infection that makes it hard to breathe and often causes coughing and fever.
- **Psychology:** The study of the mind and behavior, exploring how people think, feel, and act.
- **Pseudonym:** A fake name used by an author or artist instead of their real name.
- **Psalm:** A sacred song or poem used in worship, especially in Christian and Jewish religions.
- **Psychic:** Relating to the mind's abilities that cannot be explained by science, such as predicting the future or talking to spirits.
- **Psychotherapy:** A method of treating mental and emotional disorders by talking about conditions and solutions with a therapist.
- **Pterodactyl:** An extinct type of dinosaur that had wings and flew.
- **Receipt:** A written or printed statement acknowledging that something has been paid for or received.

Activity 1: Spell and Write

Cupboard _____ _____

Coup _____ _____

Pneumonia _____ _____

Psychology _____ _____

Pseudonym _____ _____

The Greek "p", known as "pi".

Psalm _____ _____

Psychic _____ _____

Psychotherapy _____ _____

Pterodactyl _____ _____

Receipt _____ _____

Lesson 17: The Silent "gh"

It's time to explore words with the silent "gh." Did you know that the silent "gh" originates from Old and Middle English? During the Norman Conquest, which introduced many French words into the English language, the pronunciation of "gh" softened until it eventually became silent.

In the next activity, begin by reading the definitions of the most common words containing the silent "gh." Then, practice writing each word once.

Words with the silent "gh" and their definitions:

- **Though:** Although, even if.
- **Through:** From one end or side to the other.
- **Thorough** - Complete with regard to every detail; not superficial or partial.
- **Thought** - An idea or opinion produced by thinking, or occurring suddenly in the mind.
- **Borough** - A town or district that is an administrative unit, in particular.
- **Dough** - A thick, malleable mixture of flour and liquid, used for baking into bread or pastry.
- **Bought** - Past and past participle of buy.
- **Naught** - Nothing.
- **Furlough** - A leave of absence, especially that granted to a member of the armed services.
- **Sought** - Past and past participle of seek.
- **Brought** - Past and past participle of bring.
- **Daughter** - A female offspring in relation to her parents.
- **Night** - The period from sunset to sunrise in each twenty-four hours.

Activity 1: Spell and Write.

Though _____   Naught _____

Through _____   Furlough _____

Thorough _____   Sought _____

Thought _____   Brought _____

Borough _____   Daughter _____

Dough _____   Night _____

Bought _____

LESSON 18: Doubling Final Consonants

Have you ever wondered why we sometimes double up on consonants in words like "butter" and "planner"? Double consonants in English often appear to mark a short vowel sound before them. It's like a little signal saying, "Hey, the vowel sound before me is short, so hold your horses!"

For example, in the word "hopping," the double "p" tells you to keep the "o" short, unlike "hoping," where the single "p" lets the "o" stretch out a bit longer. Now, let's explore the most important rules of consonant doubling, starting with the final consonant in a word, to better understand how they affect pronunciation and spelling.

Rule 1: Short Vowel Before a Consonant

If a word has a short vowel sound followed by a consonant, and you want to add a suffix that starts with a vowel, like "-ing" and "-ed," you double the consonant.

Short Vowel Sound	+	Suffix	=	Double Consonant
Sl**a**m		ing		sla**mm**ing
		ed		sla**mm**ed
Ref**e**r		ing		refe**rr**ing
		ed		refe**rr**ed
Regr**e**t		ing		regre**tt**ing
		ed		regre**tt**ed
Occ**u**r		ing		occu**rr**ing
		ed		occu**rr**ed
Pl**o**t		ing		plo**tt**ing
		ed		plo**tt**ed

But there are some exceptions to this rule:
- vis**i**t - vis**i**ted - vis**i**ting
- prohib**i**t - prohib**i**ting - prohib**i**ted

Note that the "i" in "visit" and "prohibit" is short, but the doubling consonant rule **does not apply**.

43

Note how words that <u>do not end with a consonant</u> and are <u>preceded by a long vowel</u> do not follow the doubling rule:

creat**e** - creating - created
explor**e** - exploring - explored
contribut**e** - contributing - contributed

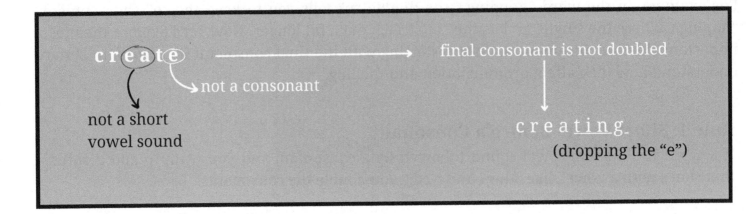

Words that are followed by <u>a suffix beginning with a consonant</u> do not follow the doubling consonant rule:

forget - forget**f**ul but forge**tt**ing
defer - defer**m**ent but deferr**i**ng

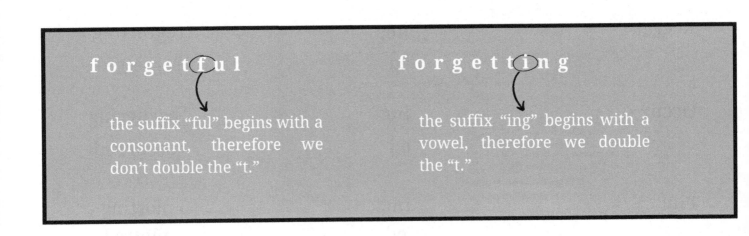

Activity 1: Add the suffixes "ing" and "ed" to the following words, to practice the first rule of doubling consonants.

	+ ing	+ ed
Refer	-----------------	-----------------
Prefer	-----------------	-----------------
Begin	-----------------	*not applicable
Control	-----------------	-----------------
Commit	-----------------	-----------------
Admit	-----------------	-----------------
Permit	-----------------	-----------------
Regret	-----------------	-----------------
Equip	-----------------	-----------------
Expel	-----------------	-----------------
Compel	-----------------	-----------------

not applicable because the past tense is irregular - "began."

Review the definitions of the words just practiced:
- **Refer:** To mention or speak about someone or something.
- **Prefer:** To like one thing or choice better than others.
- **Begin:** To start doing something.
- **Control:** To have power over something or someone.
- **Commit:** To promise to do something or to be dedicated to an activity or cause.
- **Admit:** To agree that something is true, especially unwillingly.
- **Permit:** To allow something to happen.
- **Regret:** To feel sorry or sad about a past action or mistake.
- **Equip:** To provide with the necessary materials, tools, or information.
- **Expel:** To force someone to leave a place or organization.
- **Compel:** To force or strongly persuade someone to do something.

Now that we understand when to double the final consonant when adding "-ing" and "-ed," let's explore the cases where this rule does not apply. There are two important rules that dictate when the final consonant should not be doubled.

Rule 1: when the word ends in "ch," "sh," or "ck."

		+ ing	+ ed
Words ending in "ch"	teach	teaching	*not applicable**
	reach	reaching	reached
	preach	preaching	preached
	bleach	bleaching	bleached
	snatch	snatching	snatched
Words ending in "sh"	accomplish	accomplishing	accomplished
	vanish	vanishing	vanished
	relish	relishing	relished
	demolish	demolishing	demolished
	polish	polishing	polished
Words ending in "ck"	attack	attacking	attacked
	track	tracking	tracked
	pack	packing	packed
	crack	cracking	cracked
	knock	knocking	knocked

*not applicable because the past tense is irregular - "taught."

Rule 2: when the word contains a double vowel, for example "ee," "ie," "ou," "ai," "ea" etc., and ends with a consonant.

		+ ing	+ ed
Words with a double vowel	feed	feeding	*not applicable**
	proceed	proceeding	proceeded
	appear	appearing	appeared
	bleed	bleeding	*not applicable**
	succeed	succeeding	succeeded
	gleam	gleaming	gleamed

not applicable because the past tense is irregular - "fed" and "bled."

Activity 2: Add the suffixes "ing" and "ed" to the following words, by applying all the rules on doubling learned so far. Then review the definitions of the words practiced.

	+ ing	+ ed
Occur	_____	_____
Encroach	_____	_____
Rebel	_____	_____
Concur	_____	_____
Handpick	_____	_____
Vanquish	_____	_____
Perceive	_____	_____
Auction	_____	_____
Claim	_____	_____

47

Definitions:

- **Occur:** To happen or take place.
- **Encroach:** To gradually move or go into an area that is beyond acceptable limits.
- **Rebel** *(verb):* To resist authority, control, or tradition.
- **Concur:** To agree or have the same opinion.
- **Handpick:** To select or choose something or someone with great care.
- **Vanquish:** To defeat someone or something completely in a competition or battle.
- **Perceive:** To notice or become aware of something.
- **Auction:** A public sale where goods or property are sold to the highest bidder.
- **Claim** *(verb):* To state something as true, often without providing evidence or proof.

LESSON 19: The Single and Double "l"

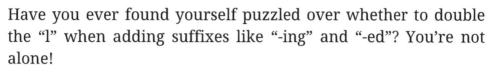

Have you ever found yourself puzzled over whether to double the "l" when adding suffixes like "-ing" and "-ed"? You're not alone!

So, what's the deal with doubling the "l"? This decision often perplexes writers and can seem like a minor detail, yet this long and slim letter can cause significant confusion. Whether a word doubles its "l" depends on a few key rules, which we'll explore to help clear up any uncertainty.

Before diving into the key rules for using a double "l" or single "l," we must first understand **syllable stress**. Syllable stress—**the emphasis placed on a particular syllable within a word**—is crucial for navigating many spelling rules. Knowing which syllable is stressed helps us decide whether to double the "l" when adding suffixes like "-ing" or "-ed." This understanding is fundamental, not only for this particular rule but for mastering the intricacies of English pronunciation and spelling generally. We will be practicing more syllables in the next part of this book.

If you're unsure of any word definitions in this lesson, refer to the glossary at the end of this lesson.

Let's train our ears to recognize different syllable stresses in words, laying the groundwork for understanding our next spelling rule:

- Cancel - (**CAN**-cel) - Stress on the first syllable.

- Control - (con-**TROL**) - Stress on the second syllable.

- Rebel - (re-**BEL**) as a verb - Stress on the second syllable.

- Label - (**LA**-bel) - Stress on the first syllable.

- Channel - (**CHAN**-nel) - Stress on the first syllable.

- Arrival - (ar-**RIV**-al) - Stress on the second syllable.

- Recital - (re-**CIT**-al) - Stress on the second syllable.

- Travel - (**TRAV**-el) - Stress on the first syllable.

49

Rule 1: if the last syllable of the word, where the "l" sits, is stressed when speaking, then double the "l" when adding endings like "-ing" or "-ed."

Stressed last syllable		+ ing	+ ed
compel	PEL	compelling	compelled
repel	PEL	repelling	repelled
expel	PEL	expelling	expelled
rebel	BEL	rebelling	rebelled
propel	PEL	propelling	propelled
extol	TOL	extolling	extolled

Exceptions: although the stress falls on the last syllable of the words "ap<u>peal</u>," "un<u>seal</u>," and "re<u>peal</u>," they do not double the "l" when adding "-ing" and "-ed." You will note that words ending in "-<u>eal</u>" do not generally double the "l" when a suffix is added to them.

appealing - appealed   unsealing - unsealed   repealing - repealed

Unstressed last syllable		+ ing	+ ed
travel	EL	traveling	traveled
cancel	CEL	canceling	canceled
label	BEL	labeling	labeled
model	DEL	modeling	modeled
signal	NAL	signaling	signaled
marshal	SHAL	marshaling	marshaled
quarrel	REL	quarreling	quarreled
revel	EL	reveling	reveled
shovel	EL	shoveling	shoveled
counsel	SEL	counseling	counseled
fuel	EL	fueling	fueled
refuel	EL	refueling	refueled

Rule 2: if a word ends in double "l," the double "l" remains unchanged when adding suffixes like "-ing" and "-ed."

End in double "l"	+ ing	+ ed
resell	reselling	*not applicable**
outsell	outselling	*not applicable**
retell	retelling	*not applicable**
recall	recalling	recalled
instill	instilling	instilled
distill	distilling	distilled
enthrall	enthralling	enthralled

not applicable because the past tense is irregular - "resold," "outsold," "retold."

Activity 1: Add the suffixes "-ing" and "-ed" to the following words, applying the rules for using single or double "l" that we have learned so far.

	+ ing	+ ed
Cancel	_____	_____
Control	_____	_____
Rebel *(verb)*	_____	_____
Label	_____	_____
Channel	_____	_____
Travel	_____	_____
Model	_____	_____
Unseal	_____	_____

	+ ing	+ ed
Resell	_____	_____ *
Compel	_____	_____
Signal	_____	_____
Marshal	_____	_____
Outsell	_____	_____ *
Extol	_____	_____
Propel	_____	_____
Appeal	_____	_____
Retell	_____	_____ *
Quarrel	_____	_____
Revel	_____	_____
Recall	_____	_____
Repeal	_____	_____
Shovel	_____	_____
Repel	_____	_____
Instill	_____	_____
Counsel	_____	_____
Expel	_____	_____
Fuel	_____	_____
Distill	_____	_____
Enthrall	_____	_____
Refuel	_____	_____

*not applicable because the past tense is irregular - "resold," "outsold," "retold."

Vocabulary Glossary

A

Appeal *(verb)*: To make a serious or urgent request, typically to the public.

C

Cancel: To decide or announce that a planned event will not take place.
Channel *(verb)*: To direct or guide something through a specific path or medium.
Compel: To force or oblige someone to do something.
Control: To have the power to direct or manage something or someone.
Counsel *(verb)*: To give advice or guidance to someone.

D

Distill: To purify a liquid by heating and cooling.

E

Enthrall: To captivate or charm someone completely.
Expel: To officially force someone to leave a place or organization.
Extol: To praise something or someone highly.

F

Fuel: To supply or power something, especially with gas or oil.

I

Instill: To gradually but firmly establish an idea or attitude into a person's mind.

L

Label: To attach a tag or name to something to identify or describe it.

M

Marshal *(verb)*: To organize or arrange things or people into order.
Model *(verb)*: To show or demonstrate something as an example for others to follow.

O

Outsell: To sell more than another product or competitor.

P

Propel: To push or drive something forward.

Q

Quarrel: To argue or disagree with someone in an angry way.

R

Rebel: To fight against or refuse to obey authority.
Recall: To remember something from the past or to officially request that a product be returned.
Refuel: To replenish the fuel supply of a vehicle or machine.
Repeal: To officially cancel a law or an act.
Repel: To drive away or resist effectively.
Resell: To sell something that you have bought to someone else.
Retell - To tell a story or event again or in a different way.
Revel: To take great pleasure or delight in something.

S

Shovel: To lift and move dirt, snow, or other materials using a tool with a broad flat blade.
Signal (verb): To make a gesture or sound to convey information or give a command.

T

Travel: To go from one place to another, often over a long distance.

U

Unseal: To open something that was closed or sealed.

LESSON 20: The "f" Sound in "f," "ph," and "gh"

Did you know the "f" sound in English can be written in many ways, depending on the word's origins and the position of the sound within the word? You might recognize the "f" sound in words like "calf" and "cough," as well as in "bluff" and "laugh." It even appears in words such as "photography," "phoenix," and "phantom."

So, how do we determine which letters to use for the "f" sound in different words? It can be written as "f," "ff," "gh," or "ph," based on the word's roots and some useful spelling rules.

Using "f"

The single "f" is commonly used in native English words and is the most straightforward representation of the "f" sound. Let's have a look at some examples containing "f" in different positions in the words:

- Fathom
- Feign
- Fester
- Aftershock
- Flourish
- Forsake
- Lifeline
- Falter
- Foster
- Befriend
- Waft

Using a single "f"

The single "f" is commonly used in words under several conditions:

- with a long vowel sound followed by the "f" sound. Examples include "leaf," "chief," "thief," "proof," "roof," "relief," and "belief." These words have long vowels directly before the "f."

- with a short vowel sound when "f" is followed by a consonant, for example, "lift," "draft," "soft," "fifty," "craft," "cleft," "shift," "loft," "drift," and "cauliflower." In these words, a short vowel is followed by an "f" and then another consonant.

- with a consonant followed by the "f" sound. Examples include "shelf," "surf," "scarf," "wharf," "wolf," "gulf," "turf," and "half." In these words, the "f" follows directly after a consonant.

Using a single "f"

Long Vowel Sound + "f"	
Leaf	ea + f
Thief	ie + f
Proof	oo + f
Relief	ie + f

Consonant + "f"	
Shelf	l + f
Surf	r + f
Scarf	r + f
Wharf	r + f
Gulf	l + f
Half	l + f

Short Vowel Sound + "f" + consonant	
Lift	i + f + t
Draft	a + f + t
Cauliflower	i + f + l
Fifty	i + f + t
Cleft	e + f + t

Using "ff"

The double "f" ("ff") is commonly used in words under the following conditions:

- at the end of a single-syllable word following a short vowel sound. Examples include "huff," "puff," "sniff," "stiff," "staff."

- in the middle of a word following a short vowel sound, for example, "waffle," "duffle," "scuffle," "muffin," "traffic," "coffee," "offering."

duffle

coffee

offering

Short Vowel Sound + "f" in the middle
u + ff (le)
o + ff (ee)
o + ff (ering)

Using "ph"

"Ph" is typically used in words of Greek origin. This usage aligns with the Greek letter "phi" (Φ), which is transliterated as "ph" in English. Words with "ph" are usually more technical or scientific in nature. Let's have a look at some examples:

- Physics
- Photosynthesis
- Phonograph
- Philosophy
- Metaphor
- Pharmacology
- Phobia

Using "gh"

The "gh" in English words such as "enough," "cough," and "laugh" traces its origins back to the Old English and Middle English periods. During this time, English evolved significantly, influenced first by Norse languages during the Viking invasions and later by Norman French following the Norman Conquest of 1066. These influences notably affected the pronunciation and spelling of many words.

Originally, the "gh" represented a sound similar to the German or Dutch "ch" as in "Bach," which is a voiceless velar fricative—a sound not commonly used in modern English. This sound proved challenging for English speakers to pronounce consistently, especially in certain dialects. Over time, in specific words and contexts, this "gh" sound either became silent or transformed into the "f" sound, depending on its position in a word and the regional English dialect.

Let's have a look at the most commonly used words containing "gh" that sounds like an "f."

- **Cough**   • **Laugh**
- **Enough**   • **Trough**
- **Tough**   • **Slough**
- **Rough**

Note that "slough" can also be spelled as "sluff" but it is less common.

Note: The term "draught" is used in British English to refer to beer drawn from a keg, among other meanings. In American English, this term is commonly spelled as "draft."

Activity 1: Below are words that contain the "f" sound, but the letters representing this sound are incorrect. Correctly spell each word using "f," "ff," "ph," or "gh," as appropriate, based on the rules we've discussed.

Phathom   _____

Pheign   _____

cofee   _____

Enouff   _____

Touph   _____

Mufin   _____

Stif   _____

Wafle   _____

Wharph   _____

Ofering   _____

Wapht   _____

Phorsake   _____

Lauph   _____

Trouph   _____

Huf   _____

Puf   _____

Scufle   _____

Trafic   _____

Fysics   _____

Filosofy   _____

Fotosynthesis   _____

Vocabulary Glossary

Single "f"
- **Fathom:** To understand something after much thought.
- **Feign:** To pretend to feel or be affected by something.
- **Fester:** To become worse or more intense, especially through long-term neglect or indifference.
- **Aftershock:** A smaller earthquake following the main shock of a large earthquake.
- **Flourish:** To grow or develop in a healthy or vigorous way.
- **Forsake:** To abandon or give up something.
- **Lifeline:** Something that provides help or support, crucial for success or survival.
- **Falter:** To lose strength or momentum.
- **Foster:** To encourage the development of something, especially something desirable.
- **Befriend:** To act as a friend to someone.
- **Waft:** To move lightly through the air.
- **Relief:** A feeling of reassurance and relaxation following stress.
- **Draft:** A preliminary version of a piece of writing.
- **Craft:** An activity involving skill in making things by hand.
- **Cleft:** A split or opening made by cracking.
- **Wharf:** A platform built on the shore that extends from the land over water, used for docking ships.
- **Gulf:** A large area of the sea partially enclosed by land.

Double "f" ("ff")
- **Huff:** To blow out loudly; a fit of anger.
- **Stiff:** Not easily bent or changed in shape; rigid.
- **Staff:** The group of people who work for an organization.
- **Duffle:** A large bag made of thick fabric, typically used for carrying personal belongings.
- **Scuffle:** A short, confused fight or struggle at close quarters.

"Ph" sounding as "f"
- **Physics:** The branch of science concerned with the nature and properties of matter and energy.
- **Photosynthesis:** The process by which green plants and some other organisms use sunlight to synthesize foods from carbon dioxide and water.
- **Phonograph:** A machine that reproduces sound from a rotating disk with grooves that a needle traces.
- **Philosophy:** The study of the fundamental nature of knowledge, reality, and existence.
- **Metaphor:** A figure of speech where a word or phrase is applied to an object or action to which it is not literally applicable.
- **Pharmacology:** The branch of medicine concerned with the uses, effects, and modes of action of drugs.
- **Phobia:** An extreme or irrational fear of or aversion to something.

"Gh" sounding as "f"
- **Trough:** A long, narrow open container for animals to eat or drink out of.
- **Slough:** An area of soft, muddy ground; swamp or swamplike region.
- **Slough** *(verb)*: To shed or remove a layer of dead skin, or to cast off something that is no longer wanted or needed.

Part 3

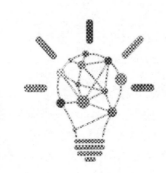

Syllables:

THE FOUNDATIONS OF ACCURATE SPELLING

LESSON 21: What are Syllables?

 A syllable is like a single beat in music. It is part of a word that you say in one beat. It usually has a vowel sound and is surrounded by consonants, which are the other letters. For example, the word "administer" has four syllables: ***ad/min/is/ter***. Do you notice the beat?

How are Syllables connected to Sound?

Every syllable of a word produces its own sound which contributes to the overall sound of the word. When we pronounce a word, we are combining different sounds to form syllables. So, when we dive into spelling and speaking, we're really tuning into the symphony of syllables that make language come to life.

Why is it Important to Learn Syllable Spelling?

1. When you practice syllable spelling, it develops your ability to hear, identify, and manipulate individual sounds in spoken words.

2. When you focus on the sound of each part of the word, it helps you develop your listening, speaking and reading skills because you become more attuned to the sound patterns within words.

3. When you break down a word into smaller parts, it helps you organize it better in your mind. This makes it easier for you to remember how to spell the word.

Important Note

In this part of the book, we are going to practice syllabification, that is, spelling in syllables, using the words we have already encountered in previous lessons and whose definitions you reviewed on pages 23-25. This will prepare you for later parts of the book, where we will practice their spelling and usage in sentences and writing.

Feel the Beat: Read the words aloud and catch their rhythm.

mys - te - ri - ous

spec - tac - u - lar

me - ta - mor - pho - sis

har - mo - ni - ca

ca - tas - tro - phe

Definitions
Mysterious: *Not easily explained.*
Spectacular: *Amazing or impressive.*
Metamorphosis: *A dramatic transformation.*
Harmonica: *A small musical instrument.*
Catastrophe: *A big disaster.*

Activity 1: Let's practice slicing words into syllables.

Acknowledge	ac - knowl - edge	_____
Administer	ad - min - is - ter	_____
Amiable	a - mi - a - ble	_____
Antagonize	an - tag - o - nize	_____
Apprehend	ap - pre - hend	_____
Catalyst	cat - a - lyst	_____
Fallacy	fal - la - cy	_____
Malady	mal - a - dy	_____
Acre	a - cre	_____
Alien	a - li - en	_____
Debate	de - bate	_____
Fable	fa - ble	_____
Salient	sa - li - ent	_____

Activity 2: Which of the following words has only ONE syllable? You can circle or underline them.

Ache	Debate
Acre	Fable
Alien	Salient
Crave	Wane

Activity 3: Which 5 words from the previous exercise have more than one syllable?

_____

_____

_____

_____

_____

Activity 4: Let's practice some more sounds by splitting the words into syllables.

Detail	de - tail	_____
Equilibrium	e - qui - lib - ri - um	_____
Problem	prob - lem	_____
Facade	fa - cade	_____
Extreme	ex - treme	_____
Severe	se - vere	_____
Epidemic	ep - i - dem - ic	_____
Independent	in - de - pend - ent	_____
Endurance	en - dur - ance	_____
Maneuver	ma - neu - ver	_____
Enemy	en - e - my	_____
Envision	en - vi - sion	_____
Item	i - tem	_____

LESSON 22: Syllables Guide Sound Patterns

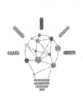

Did you know that breaking down words into syllables helps you pronounce words more accurately? Syllables provide a clear guide to the sound pattern, known as phonetic structure, of words. This is especially beneficial when words sound unfamiliar or complex. Let's break down into syllables some intriguing words encountered in previous lessons.

Notice how each part of the word contributes to its overall pronunciation. By practicing this technique, you'll find it easier to tackle any word, no matter how complicated it appears at first glance. When you break down challenging words into syllables they look less intimidating and easier to remember. This will also help pinpoint the exact location of those elusive letters within each word. Ready to dive in? Let's go!

Activity 1: Match the syllables in the puzzle pieces to form complete words.

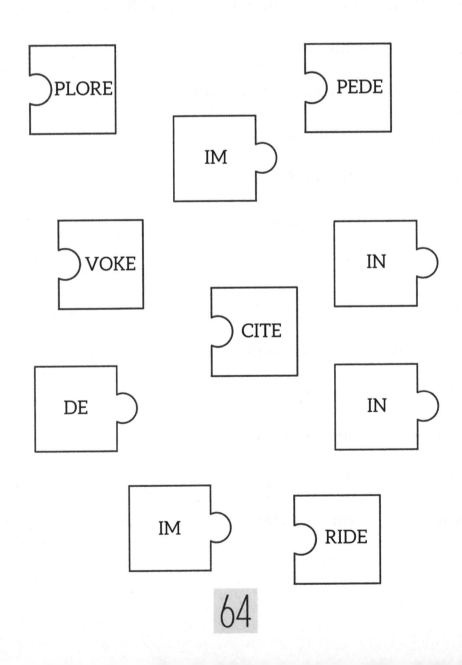

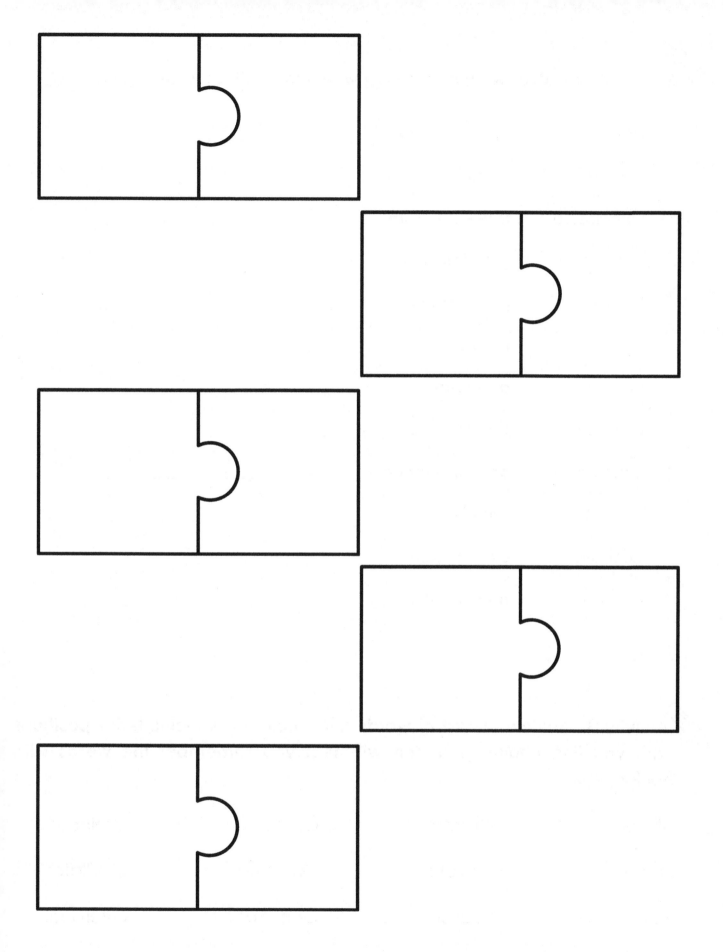

Activity 2: Break down the following words into syllables, as shown.

Alimony	al - i - mo - ny	_____
Erosion	e - ro - sion	_____
Foreclosure	fore - clo - sure	_____
Grotesque	gro - tesque	_____
Provoke	pro - voke	_____
Robust	ro - bust	_____
Obscure	ob - scure	_____
Obsolete	ob - so - lete	_____
Occurrence	oc - cur - rence	_____
Ominous	om - i - nous	_____
Oscillate	os - cil - late	_____
Overdue	o - ver - due	_____

Activity 3: Review the list of words and circle the specific letter positions that you find challenging. This will help you remember the words with tricky letters.

Alimony	Grotesque	Obscure	Ominous
Erosion	Provoke	Obsolete	Oscillate
Foreclosure	Robust	Occurrence	Overdue

Activity 4: Break down the following words into syllables, as shown.

Fundamental **fun - da - ment - tal** _____

Unique **u - nique** _____

Amuse **a - muse** _____

Succumb **suc - cumb** _____

Judgment **judg - ment** _____

Humane **hu - mane** _____

Rupture **rup - ture** _____

Refuse **re - fuse** _____

Accuse **ac - cuse** _____

Nurture **nur - ture** _____

Consumable **con - sum - a - ble** _____

Plummet **plum - met** _____

 Remember that the letter "b" in "succumb" is silent and not pronounced.

Part 4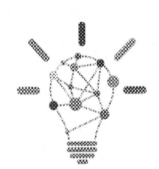

Spelling Practice and Word Usage

LESSON 23: Words in Context

Learning to spell is not just about remembering letters. It is also about understanding how to use words in sentences. Every word has its meaning, and we use words to share our thoughts and ideas clearly.

When you practice spelling, it's important to also learn how to use these words in the right context. The activities we will do next are designed to help you not only spell the targeted words correctly but also use them appropriately in sentences.

In this part of the book we will be practicing the spelling and word usage of the words already introduced in Parts 1 and 2. When in doubt, you can review the definitions of these words by referring to the glossaries on pages 23-25, 53 and 59.

Activity 1: Choose the best definition for each word.

Acknowledge:
a) to reject or deny
b) to admit the existence or truth of
c) to consider carefully
d) to decorate with colors

Antagonize:
a) to work together harmoniously
b) to oppose or provoke anger in
c) to form a clear mental image of
d) to take by force

Administer:
a) to establish a new rule
b) to take away power from
c) to manage or direct the execution of
d) to ignore completely

Apprehend:
a) To understand or perceive something mentally.
b) To anticipate or fear something.
c) To arrest or take someone into custody.
d) To physically grasp or seize something.

Amiable:
a) friendly and pleasant
b) difficult to understand
c) causing anger or irritation
d) lacking energy

Catalyst:
a) a substance that speeds up a chemical reaction
b) a long journey for a specific purpose
c) an argument or disagreement
d) a type of wild animal

Fallacy:
a) a mistaken belief, especially one based on unsound arguments
b) an essential truth or law
c) a small, secluded room
d) a written record of historical events

Malady:
a) a contagious disease
b) a severe storm or hurricane
c) a state of happiness and contentment
d) a sudden and violent emotional reaction

Paradigm:
a) a perfect example or model
b) a complicated mathematical problem
c) a feeling of great pleasure
d) a type of musical instrument

Activity 2: Choose the word for each situation which best describes the underlined words or phrases.

Ache Acre Alien Crave Debate Fable Salient Wane

1. While watching a mystery movie, **one peculiar detail** about the villain's love for polka-dotted socks seems to stick out oddly.

----

2. You're reading a hilarious <u>tale</u> about a tortoise who tries to cheat in a race against the hare by using a skateboard.

----

3. "**Should pets be allowed to run for president**?"

70

Ache Acre Alien Crave Debate Fable Salient Wane

4. You've just inherited a **large piece of land** from a distant relative, big enough to fit a small soccer field.

----

5. Last night you dreamed of mountains made of spaghetti and rivers of chocolate and **that's all you can think about** right now.

----

6. In your backyard, you find a spaceship the size of a toaster. **The pilot**? A creature with three eyes, who asks you for directions to the nearest donut shop.

----

7. After trying to break the world record for most jumping jacks in one minute, you discover parts of your body you never knew could feel <u>sore</u>!

----

8. After the excitement of your birthday party, the energy in the room slowly <u>starts to decrease</u> as guests begin to leave.

71

LESSON 24: Spell Quest

 Repeating words several times might seem boring, but it's actually a really important way to get better at spelling. When you understand why you're doing it, it becomes less of a chore.

Each time you spell a word, you're training your brain to remember it. Think of it like practicing a sport or a video game – the more you do it, the better you get. So, when we repeat spelling, it's not just to keep you busy; it's to help you become a spelling champ!

✏️ Activity 1: Spell and Write

Acknowledge _____ _____

Administer _____ _____

Amiable _____ _____

Antagonize _____ _____

Apprehend _____ _____

Catalyst _____ _____

Fallacy _____ _____

Malady _____ _____

Ache _____ _____

Acre _____ _____

Alien _____ _____

Crave _____ _____

Debate _____ _____

Fable _____ _____

Salient _____ _____

Wane _____ _____

LESSON 25: Inferring Word Meaning in Context

 Words are like keys. They unlock meanings and paint a picture in our minds. We're going to explore some more Tier 2 words that we encountered in the previous lessons by practicing their definitions and usage in writing.

Activity 1: Read and Answer

He was an athlete known for his **extreme** sports. He dedicated his life to conquering the world's most daunting mountain peaks. His **endurance** was legendary; he could cross icy ridges and climb steep cliffs in **severe** weather conditions for hours. His secret lay not just in his physical strength but in his extraordinary mental **equilibrium**. He approached each challenge with calmness and maintained a balance between pushing his limits and respecting nature's power.

1. What do you think is "**extreme**" about this sport?

----

2. Choose the best words that mean "**endurance**" in this context:
i.   stamina
ii. strength
iii. fearlessness
iv. timeliness

3. What is the **opposite** of "severe weather conditions":
i.   harsh weather
ii. mild weather
iii. stormy weather

4. Find a word in the text that means "**equilibrium**."

73

5. In your own words, what is this story about?

✏️ **Activity 2: Read and Answer**

During my visit to France, I could not help but **envision** myself as a character in a historical novel, wandering through streets lined with buildings whose **facades** spoke of a rich and tumultuous past. Each **detail** of the ornate architecture seemed to whisper stories of times when these walls might have hidden friends from **enemies**, or seen secret **maneuvers** of resistance fighters claiming their **independent** land.

1. Which word best substitutes "**envision**"?
A) see
B) imagine
C) view

2. The building facades in France are mentioned as having:
    A) Bright, modern colors.
    B) Minimalist designs.
    C) Stories of historical significance.
    D) No aesthetic appeal.

3. The term "**<u>independent</u>**" in the context of the narrative refers to:
    A) The narrator's travel style.
    B) France's famous landmarks.
    C) The spirit of resistance fighters.
    D) The narrator's decision to dine alone.

4. The narrator specifically identifies who the **<u>enemies</u>** were in the history of France.
    • True
    • False

5. The use of "**<u>maneuver</u>**" implies that historical actions in France were always peaceful.
    • True
    • False

6. Focusing on architectural **<u>details</u>** helps the narrator feel connected to France's history.
    • True
    • False

LESSON 26: Spell Quest

How does correct spelling connect us to others? Correct spelling helps ensure our written message is understood by everyone. By spelling words correctly we bridge gaps and build understanding. Spelling is a tool for clarity, but also for creativity. It allows us to paint pictures with words, evoke emotions, and convey ideas.

Activity 1: Can you find the misspelled words and write down its correct spelling?

1. In the midst of battle, Sergeant Lucas showed remarkable andurence. He led a manoover that was crucial for his team's survival. It was a challenging day, marked by seveer and extreem conditions which tested the soldiers' physical and mental limits.

A._____

B._____

C._____

D._____

2. In a physics classroom, the gravity pendulum served as a fascinating itim of study. The teacher showed every detael of it, like how long its string was and how heavy the bottom part was. This pendulum helped students see its dynamic ekwilibreum in action, as it passed to its lowest point when swinging from side to side.

A._____

B._____

C._____

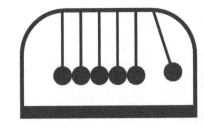

3. The small town faced a sever problem when an epidemmic of flu swept through, escalating quickly from a handful of cases to an extream public health crisis.

A._____

B._____

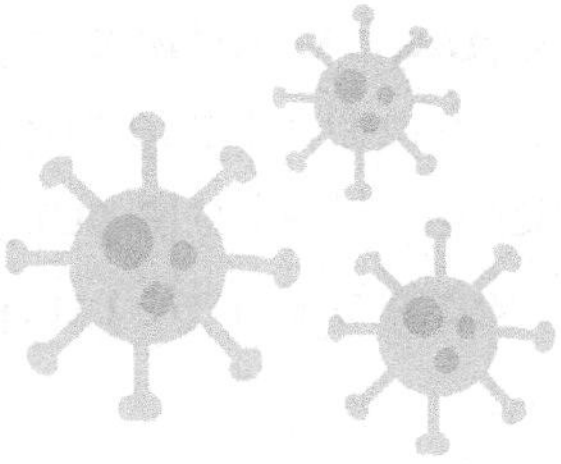

C._____

Activity 2: Take a look at the words we've practiced in the previous lessons. Pick out any words that you feel you need more practice with. Write these words down twice in the spaces provided below. This will help you focus on the words that are a bit tricky for you.

Detail   _____   _____

Equilibrium   _____   _____

Problem   _____   _____

Facade   _____   _____

Extreme   _____   _____

Severe   _____   _____

Epidemic   _____   _____

Independent   _____   _____

Endurance   _____   _____

Maneuver   _____   _____

Enemy   _____   _____

Envision   _____   _____

Item   _____   _____

Activity 3: For each sentence, choose the option that best rephrases and explains the action described by the underlined word.

1. Seeing the little puppy in distress, Sarah <u>implored</u> her parents to let her adopt it.
A) Seeing the little puppy in distress, Sarah looked at her parents with hope.
B) Seeing the little puppy in distress, Sarah begged her parents to let her adopt it.
C) Seeing the little puppy in distress, Sarah told her parents about it later.

2. The heavy traffic would <u>impede</u> their arrival at the concert, making them worry they'd miss the opening act.
A) The heavy traffic made them drive faster to the concert.
B) The heavy traffic had no effect on their excitement about the concert.
C) The heavy traffic made them slow and possibly late for the concert.

3. During the trial, the defense lawyer <u>invoked</u> the Fourth Amendment to argue that the evidence against his client was obtained through an illegal search and seizure.
A) A) During the trial, the defense lawyer mentioned the Fourth Amendment arguing it was obtained illegally.
B) During the trial, the defense lawyer cited the Fourth Amendment arguing it was obtained illegally.
C) During the trial, the defense lawyer briefly talked about the Fourth Amendment arguing it was obtained illegally.

4. The class clown often tried to <u>deride</u> the substitute teacher's accent.
A) The class clown often mimicked the substitute teacher's accent.
B) The class clown often praised the substitute teacher's accent.
C) The class clown often made fun of the substitute teacher's accent.

5. The rumor about the haunted library began to <u>incite</u> curiosity among the students, leading them to explore it after dark.
A) The rumor about the haunted library made students avoid it after dark.
B) The rumor about the haunted library made students curious, so they went to see it after dark.
C) The rumor about the haunted library confused the students about its location.

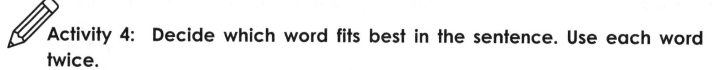

Activity 4: Decide which word fits best in the sentence. Use each word twice.

Invoke   Implore   Impede   Deride   Incite

1. It's not kind to _____ someone's dreams, no matter how unrealistic they may seem; everyone has the right to aspire towards their goals without fear of mockery.

2. When the community faced unjust laws, the leader often _____ ancient rights that protected the people, showing that history still had power in modern times.

3. Sensational news stories don't just inform the public; sometimes, they _____ panic or unrest, leading to unnecessary chaos in the community.

4. The heavy snowfall not only made the roads slippery; it _____ all travel, making it nearly impossible for vehicles to pass through the mountainous region.

5. Faced with the possibility of losing his home, the man _____ the bank manager to give him more time to pay his mortgage.

6. The child _____ his mother to buy him a new video game, promising to do extra chores around the house.

7. The controversial article did not provide new information but managed to _____ a heated debate among readers on social media.

8. A broken-down car in the single-lane tunnel _____ traffic during rush hour, causing long delays.

9. The lawyer _____ the self-defense statute to protect his client from charges, emphasizing the right to personal safety.

10. Critics often _____ the latest fashion trends, but they quickly become popular among the youth.

Activity 5: Read each sentence and decide the definition of the underlined word from its context. Choose the correct meaning from the provided options.

1. Even when faced with unfair rules, Clara chose to **abide** by them, believing in following the system for change.
A) Ignore completely
B) Fight against
C) Follow or adhere to

2. Despite the overwhelming pressure to conform, Liam's **defiant** stance inspired others to stand up for their beliefs.
A) Fearful
B) Boldly resistant or challenging
C) Agreeable

3. The discussion about environmental policies turned into a **quagmire**, with no clear solution in sight due to conflicting interests.
A) A straightforward debate
B) A celebratory event
C) A complex, difficult situation

4. To ensure the water was safe to drink, the team used a **filter** to remove all harmful bacteria and impurities.
A) A decorative item
B) A tool for cooking food
C) A device to remove contaminants

5. The rights enshrined in the constitution were considered **<u>inviolable</u>**, meant to protect citizens under all circumstances.
A) Sacred and must not be infringed
B) Easily changed
C) Open for interpretation

6. Gazing at the **<u>immense</u>** mountain range, she felt a mix of awe and fear at the daunting challenge ahead.
A) Tiny and insignificant
B) Extremely large or vast
C) Slightly elevated

7. The unfair accusation from his colleague was enough to **<u>infuriate</u>** Alex, leading to a heated argument.
A) Calm down
B) Slightly annoy
C) Make very angry

8. The critics did not offer constructive feedback; instead, they chose to **<u>deride</u>** the artist's work, mocking its originality.
A) Ridicule
B) Praise
C) Ignore politely

Activity 6: Write down each word in the spaces provided, paying special attention to the underlined letters.

Inv̱oke	_____	_____	_____
Impl<u>ore</u>	_____	_____	_____
Imp<u>ede</u>	_____	_____	_____
<u>D</u>eride	_____	_____	_____
In<u>ci</u>te	_____	_____	_____
De<u>fia</u>nt:	_____	_____	_____
<u>Qua</u>gmire:	_____	_____	_____
Infur<u>ia</u>te:	_____	_____	_____
<u>A</u>bide:	_____	_____	_____
Inv<u>io</u>lable:	_____	_____	_____

LESSON 27: Contextual Clues to Define Words

Activity 1: Can you determine the meaning of the underlined words based on the context in which they appear? Try using your own words as much as possible.

1. After the divorce was finalized, Sarah had to budget carefully, as the monthly **alimony** from her ex-partner was now a crucial part of her income.

Definition: _____

2. Over the years, the constant **erosion** of the cliff by the sea waves caused the once-safe lookout point to become dangerous.

Definition: _____

3. Facing **foreclosure**, the Johnson family packed their belongings, heartbroken that the bank was taking their home due to missed mortgage payments.

Definition: _____

4. The old mansion's walls were covered in **grotesque** paintings that twisted and distorted the figures into shapes that seemed almost too bizarre to be art.

Definition: _____

5. Her teasing remarks were meant to **provoke** a reaction, pushing him until he couldn't help but respond in frustration.

Definition: _____

6. Despite the harsh weather conditions, the **robust** construction of the shelter kept all inside safe and warm, proving its strength and durability.

Definition: _____

Activity 2: Choose the best word for each situation.

Consumable Humane Judgment Nurture Plummet Unique

1. During the class play, the prop chandelier was supposed to lower gracefully onto the stage, but instead it took a <u>nosedive,</u> startling the audience with a sudden thud.

2. In a wild science class experiment, students make <u>edible</u> water bottles using algae and plant extracts, creating the weirdest <u>edible</u> water anyone's ever seen.

3. A young girl decides to <u>care for</u> her plants by talking to them daily; she's convinced her basil grows better when discussed the weather and latest pop songs.

4. In a family game of "Judge the Jelly Bean," where each person guesses the flavor while blindfolded, Grandpa makes a <u>critical decision</u> and declares every jelly bean to be "old sock" flavor.

----

5. Trying to set the most <u>compassionate</u> trap possible, a girl designs a spa-like retreat to catch a mouse, complete with cheese snacks and soothing music.

----

6. During a school costume contest, a student shows up dressed as a dinosaur riding a bicycle, definitely a <u>one-of-a-kind</u> costume that has everyone talking.

Activity 3: **Read each sentence and decide the definition of the underlined word from its context. Then choose the correct word from the provided options.**

1. After resisting the urge to cheat on the difficult exam, he finally **succumbed** to looking at his classmate's paper.
A) Gave in to pressure or temptation
B) Continued to resist successfully
C) Focused intensely on his own work
D) Reported the incident to the teacher

2. During the debate, Sarah openly **accused** her opponent of misrepresenting the facts.
A) Praised
B) Criticized
C) Charged with wrongdoing
D) Supported

3. Even though everyone was trying the new dish, Mia chose to **refuse** due to her dietary restrictions.

A) Accept

B) Deny

C) Decline

D) Embrace

4. Understanding the scientific method is **fundamental** to succeeding in any science course.

A) Complicated

B) Optional

C) Basic and necessary

D) Advanced

5. The old pipe in the school basement finally **ruptured**, causing a flood during the rainy season.

A) Blocked

B) Burst open

C) Leaked slowly

D) Was repaired

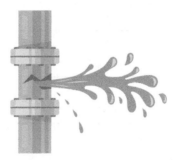

6. The witty remarks of the guest speaker managed to **amuse** the crowd, keeping everyone engaged.

A) Confuse

B) Entertain

C) Bore

D) Frighten

Activity 4: Write down each word in the space provided, paying special attention to the underlined letters.

Funda<u>a</u>mental _____ _____

Uni<u>que</u> _____ _____

<u>A</u>muse _____ _____

Suc<u>c</u>umb _____ _____

Ju<u>dg</u>ment _____ _____

Hum<u>a</u>ne _____ _____

Rup<u>tur</u>e _____ _____

Ref<u>use</u> _____ _____

Ac<u>cuse</u> _____ _____

<u>N</u>ur<u>t</u>ure _____ _____

Consum<u>able</u> _____ _____

Plum<u>met</u> _____ _____

LESSON 28: Proofreading

In our upcoming activity, you'll step into the shoes of a proofreader, embarking on a mission to uncover spelling mistakes. A proofreader meticulously reviews texts to identify and fix errors in spelling, grammar, and punctuation, ensuring a book is polished and error-free before it gets published.

Did you know that a proofreader plays a crucial role in the publishing process of a book? They act as the last line of defense before a book reaches its audience. For authors, a proofreader's eye for detail can mean the difference between a polished, professional piece of writing and one that may be perceived as sloppy or unprofessional.

Activity 1: Scan the paragraphs for spelling mistakes like a pro proofreader. Use your sharp eyes to spot and correct each error you find. Ready to show off your spelling skills? Let's get started!

1. In the wake of their recent divorce, John found himself struggling with the financial burden of allimony. The payments were often overdeu, causing tension and discomfort in his already strained relationship with his ex-spouse. This occurence became a monthly ordeal, as each missed deadline seemed to provook further arguments between them. John realized he needed to find a better way to manage his obligations to avoid these confrontations and maintain some semblance of peace.

Correction: A. _____   B. _____

C. _____   D. _____

2. As the scientist stood at the edge of the cliff, observing the erotion that had sculpted the landscape over centuries, an ominus feeling washed over her. The once roebust mountain, known for its unyielding strength, now bore the unmistakable marks of nature's relentless force. She realized that even the mightiest structures were not immune to the gradual but powerful effects of the wind and water.

Correction: A. _____   B. _____

C. _____

3. Tucked away in a corner of the museum was a grotesqeu sculpture, its exaggerated features capturing the attention of every visitor. Despite its prominence, the origins of this piece remained obbscure, shrouded in mystery and lost to time. As the day progressed, the shadow of the sculpture seemed to ossillate across the floor, driven by the shifting sunbeams through the windows and giving life to its otherwise inanimate form.

Correction: A. _____   B. _____

            C. _____

4. In the small town, the old factory facing forclosure stood as a somber reminder of times gone by. Once the heartbeat of the community, its machinery now lay silent and obsoleet, overtaken by advancements that rendered its operations redundant. The looming closure not only marked the end of an era but also signified the need for the town to adapt and find new paths forward in a rapidly changing world.

Correction: A. _____   B. _____

Part 5

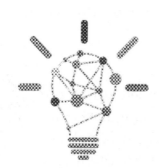

Affixes: Prefixes and Suffixes

LESSON 29: Prefixes

What Are Prefixes?

Imagine you have a magic key that can unlock new meanings for hundreds of words. That's what prefixes are like! A prefix is a group of letters that you add to the beginning of a word to change its meaning. For example, adding "un-" to "happy" makes "unhappy," which means not happy.

Where Do Prefixes Come From?

Prefixes are like little pieces of history wrapped up in our language. They come from lots of different languages like Latin and Greek. When these languages mixed with English a long time ago, they brought their prefixes with them. For example, the prefix "anti-" means "against" or "opposite," and it comes from Greek. So, when we talk about "antifreeze," it means something that works against freezing.

Why Are They Useful?

Knowing about prefixes can turn you into a word detective. By looking at the prefix, you can guess the meaning of a new word before you even look it up. This makes reading new books and learning in school much easier. For example, knowing that "bio-" relates to life (as in "biology" or "biodegradable") helps you understand that any word with this prefix will involve life in some way.

Why Do We Group Prefixes?

Grouping prefixes by themes like number, location, or time helps you to see patterns and connections among different words. This thematic grouping is not just about memorizing a list; it's about understanding the function of a prefix. When you come across a new word with a familiar prefix, you can make a good guess about its meaning. This makes reading new texts easier and more enjoyable because you're equipped with the tools to decode unfamiliar words.

Let's dive into these groups, discover the roles these prefixes play, and see how they guide us in understanding complex vocabulary. By the end of this lesson, you'll be equipped to use these prefixes as keys to unlock word meanings.

LESSON 30: Number Prefixes

 Numbers shape much of our understanding of the world, from counting objects to organizing information in order. In language, certain prefixes play a pivotal role in indicating numbers and sequences. These prefixes, known as number prefixes, help us quickly understand how many or in what order something is being discussed just by looking at the beginning of a word. For example, a "bicycle" ("bi-") has two wheels, and a "trilogy" ("tri-") consists of three parts. By learning these number prefixes, you'll gain the ability to instantly discern the numerical relationships in words, which will help you navigate and understand various subjects more clearly.

 **Activity 1: Study the table below to learn the meanings of various number prefixes, complete with examples and their definitions. This will help you understand how these prefixes are used to create words that indicate quantity or order. The most common prefixes are underlined for easy identification.**

PREFIX	MEANING	EXAMPLE WORD	DEFINITION
Mono-	one	monarchy	A form of government ruled by a single person, such as a king or queen.
Uni-	one	universe	All of space - stars, planets, and galaxies - as a single unified entity.
Bi-	two	bicycle	A vehicle with two wheels powered by pedaling.

PREFIX	MEANING	EXAMPLE WORD	DEFINITION
Di-	two	dioxide	A chemical compound containing two oxygen atoms bonded to another element.
Tri	three	triangle	A shape with three straight sides and three angles.
Quad-	four	quadrant	A quarter of a circle or a four-part division of an area.
Tetra-	four	tetrapod	A vertebrate animal with four feet or leg-like appendages.
Penta-	five	pentagon	A geometric figure with five sides and five angles.
Quint-	five	quintuplet	One of five offspring born at one birth.
Hexa-	six	hexagon	A geometric figure with six straight sides and six angles.
Sex-	six	sextet	A group of six individuals.

PREFIX	MEANING	EXAMPLE WORD	DEFINITION
Hepta-	seven	heptagon	A polygon with seven sides and seven angles.
Sept-	seven	septennial	Occurring every seven years.
Octa-	eight	octagon	A shape with eight straight sides and eight angles.
Octo-	eight	octopus	A sea creature with eight arms.
Nona-	nine	nonagon	A polygon with nine sides and nine angles.
Ennea-	nine	ennead	A group or set of nine.
Deca-	ten	decade	A period of ten years.
Multi-	many	multimedia	The use of several media (like text, audio, and video) to communicate information.

Activity 2: Read the sentences below and determine the meaning of each bolded word with a prefix from this lesson. This exercise will enhance your understanding of prefixes and improve your ability to infer meanings from context.

1. In her solo performance, Sarah held the stage alone, speaking her lengthy **monologue** without interruption from other characters.

Meaning of "monologue": _____

2. With its **monopoly** on coffee production, the company was the only source for coffee beans in the region, preventing any competitors from selling them.

Meaning of "monopoly": _____

3. His art exhibit featured **monochrome** paintings, each using only one color but in various shades.

Meaning of "monochrome": _____

4. The professor, known for his meticulous detail, peered through his **monocle** to scrutinize the fine print of ancient manuscripts.

Meaning of "monocle": _____

5. At the park, the performer skillfully rode a **unicycle**, balancing on just one wheel as he juggled colorful balls, drawing a crowd of fascinated onlookers.

Meaning of "unicycle": _____

6. The choir sang in perfect **unison**, their voices merging into one harmonious sound that filled the concert hall.

Meaning of "unison": _____

7. The **bilateral** peace talks directly engaged both countries, involving negotiations aimed at resolving longstanding conflicts.

Meaning of "bilateral": _____

_____

8. She became **bilingual** in her youth, fluently speaking both English and Spanish, which opened doors to understanding two diverse cultures.

Meaning of "bilingual": _____

9. In his lecture, the professor discussed the **dichotomy** between traditional and modern art forms, illustrating the stark differences and dual perspectives prevalent in the art community.

Meaning of "dichotomy": _____

10. Faced with a **dilemma** between pursuing a career in music or medicine, he struggled to choose just one path as each held a deep appeal.

Meaning of "dilemma": _____

11. He trained for months to prepare for the **triathlon**, an event that challenges athletes with three continuous and sequential endurance races involving swimming, cycling, and running.

Meaning of "triathlon": _____

_____

12. The park's new playground featured a large sandpit shaped like a **quadrilateral**, with four straight sides perfect for various games.

Meaning of "quadrilateral": _____

_____

13. The architecture of the new federal building was inspired by a **pentagon**, designed with five equal sides to symbolize the unity of the five branches of the military.

Meaning of "pentagon": _____

_____

14. The math teacher drew a **hexagon** on the board, explaining that it's a shape with six equal sides, commonly found in nature, like in the pattern of a turtle's shell.

Meaning of "hexagon": _____

_____

15. The mixed martial arts competition took place in an **octagonal** ring, known as the octagon, which has eight sides to provide more angles for the fighters.

Meaning of "octagonal": _____

16. Reflecting on the past **decade**, the historian noted significant changes in technology and culture.

Meaning of "decade": _____

LESSON 31: Location and Position Prefixes

 Words can often give us clues about where something is located or its position relative to other things. This is the power of location and position prefixes, small but mighty parts of words that help us express relationships in space and placement.

In this lesson, we'll be exploring a variety of intriguing prefixes that describe positions and locations. Gaining a grasp on these prefixes will enhance your vocabulary and empower you to communicate more precisely about the spatial and relational aspects of the world.

 **Activity 1: Study the table below to learn the meanings of various location and position prefixes, complete with examples and their definitions. Then complete the activity that follows.**

PREFIX	MEANING	EXAMPLE WORD	DEFINITION
Sub-	under below	subterranean	Existing, situated, or operating below the surface of the earth.
Inter-	between among	interstate	Highways that go between states.
Super-	above over	supernatural	Something that exists above or beyond natural laws.

PREFIX	MEANING	EXAMPLE WORD	DEFINITION
Sur-	above over	surcharge	An additional charge or payment.
Trans-	across through	transport	To carry something from one place to another.
Intra-	within	intrastate	Within a single state.
Exo-	outside	exoplanet	A planet that orbits a star outside our solar system.

 Activity 2: Can you think of any other words that start with these prefixes? List them below.

Sub_____

Inter_____

Super_____

Sur_____

Trans_____

Intra_____

Exo_____

Activity 3: Below are sentences with missing words, each related to a specific prefix. Use the word bank provided to fill in the blanks appropriately. This activity will help you understand how prefixes influence the meaning of words and how they are used in context.

Exodus	Interactive	Intranet	Superimpose	Surmount
Exoskeleton	Intercept	Intravenous	Superior	Surpass
Exosphere	Intermingle		Supersede	
	Intranet	Subdue	Surmount	Transcribe
	Intravenous	Submarine	Surpass	Translucent
		Subzero		

1. The research team deployed a _____ to explore the mysterious, sunken ruins deep beneath the Pacific Ocean.

2. The science museum's new _____ exhibit allows visitors to conduct virtual chemical experiments using touch screens.

3. She achieved _____ results on her project by conducting extensive research and presenting her findings clearly.

4. He had to _____ numerous obstacles on his journey to becoming a champion, including injury and defeat.

5. The artist used sheets of _____ paper in her installation to play with light and shadow, creating a mesmerizing effect.

6. The patient received an _____ drip to administer medication directly into the bloodstream for immediate effect.

7. The company's _____ was updated to facilitate better communication and resource sharing among employees.

8. Biologists examined the _____ of the beetle under a microscope to learn how it provides protection and support to the creature.

Exodus	Interactive	Intranet	Superimpose	Surmount
Exoskeleton	Intercept	Intravenous	Superior	Surpass
Exosphere	Intermingle		Supersede	
	Intranet	Subdue	Surmount	Transcribe
	Intravenous	Submarine	Surpass	Translucent
		Subzero		

9. The sudden _____ of people from the city was triggered by rumors of an impending natural disaster.

10. In the movie, the hero managed to _____ the villain using clever tactics, ensuring the city's safety.

11. The skilled goalkeeper managed to _____ the ball just as it was about to cross into the goal, saving the game.

12. In the film editing workshop, the students learned how to _____ digital effects onto live-action footage to enhance the visual impact.

13. The new software update will _____ all previous versions, providing enhanced features and better security.

14. The historian spent hours in the library, _____ ancient manuscripts to uncover forgotten histories.

15. Scientists studied the _____ behavior of viruses to understand how they replicate within human cells.

16. During their astronomy lesson, the students learned that the _____ is the outermost layer of Earth's atmosphere, where air is extremely thin.

17. During the harsh winter expedition, temperatures plunged to _____, challenging the climbers' endurance and gear.

18. At the cultural festival, the sounds of different music styles _____, creating a vibrant atmosphere.

19. Her final project _____ all expectations and set a new standard for future classes.

LESSON 32: Negation or Opposition Prefixes 1

 Have you ever noticed how adding a few letters at the beginning of a word can completely change its meaning? In English, we have special prefixes that do just that—turn a word into its opposite! These are called negation or opposition prefixes. Negation prefixes express something that isn't. For example, by adding

"un-" to "satisfactory," we get "unsatisfactory," which means something is not good enough or fails to meet the required standards. These prefixes are super handy for expressing the reverse of an idea.

In this part of the book, we'll explore negation prefixes like "un-," "in-," "im-," "il-," "ir-," "dis-," and "non-." Each of these prefixes attaches to words to negate them or express opposition. Before we begin, it is important to note that English is a language rich in history, borrowing words from many other languages like Latin, Greek, French, and German. Consequently, **there are no clear-cut rules about which negation prefixes to use with certain words.** This means that some words follow patterns due to their origins or common usage that might not apply to other words, even if they seem similar.

Instead of strict rules, what we have are guidelines based on common patterns and historical usage. These guidelines can help you guess the correct prefix most of the time, but there will always be exceptions. If you're unsure which prefix to use, the best approach is to look it up in a dictionary and practice using it as often as possible. Remember, mastering English is about practice and exposure, so keep reading, writing, and speaking!

LESSON 33: The Prefix "un-"

 The prefix "un-" is quite versatile and commonly used in English to form the opposites of adjectives and verbs, primarily indicating negation or the reversal of an action.

Refresher: **Verbs** *are words that express actions, occurrences, or states of being (run, eat, think).* **Adjectives** *are words used to describe or modify nouns or pronouns, providing more detail about their qualities, quantities, or states (blue, tall, happy).*

When the prefix "un-" is added to a verb or an adjective, it changes the meaning of the word to its opposite meaning.

Examples:
- He untied his shoelaces because they were too tight. **"Tie" is the verb and in this example it is in the Past Simple Tense.**
- Having two Ph.Ds is very uncommon. **"Common" is the adjective and by adding the prefix "un-," we intend the opposite of its meaning.**

When adding prefixes to verbs in sentences, the tenses change according to the context of the sentence. For example, "Every evening she unties her shoelaces because her feet swell." **In this example "tie" is used in the Simple Present Tense.**

Sometimes, when adding the prefix to a verb, the past participle of the verb is used.
Example: He managed to elude the robbers unseen. **"Seen" is the past participle of the verb "see."**

102

Activity 1: Review and study the provided table to understand how the prefix "un-" alters the meanings of verbs.

Base Word (verb or past participle)	Definition	Negation	Definition (negated form)
seen* (see)	To observe or notice something.	un+seen	Something that has not been seen or observed.
veil	To cover or conceal.	un+veil	To reveal or disclose.
fold	To bend over on itself.	un+fold	To open or spread out.
leash	To restrain with a rope or strap.	un+leash	To release or set free.
tie	To fasten with a knot.	un+tie	To loosen or release from ties.

*"Seen" is the past participle of "see."

Activity 2: Read each sentence carefully. Choose the correct form of the verb from the options provided (either the positive or negated form) to best complete the sentence. Fill in the blank with your chosen verb. Pay attention to the context to determine which form is appropriate.

See Veil Fold Leash Tie

1. She carefully _____ the old map along its creases to avoid tearing it.

2. The lighthouse was _____ from miles away despite the dense fog.

3.The wolf moved stealthily through the shadowy forest, remaining completely _____ by the unsuspecting hikers.

4. He quickly _____ the ropes to free the boat from the dock.

5. The magician used a cloth to _____ the cage, and when he removed it, the bird was gone.

6. He _____ his energetic puppy before walking in the park.

7. He carefully _____ the crumpled letter he found, revealing the hidden message inside.

8. She quickly _____ the boat to the dock before the storm hit.

9. The company will _____ its new product at the conference next week.

10. The sudden release of the dam waters _____ a torrent downstream.

104

Activity 3: Review and study the provided table to understand how the prefix "un-" alters the meanings of adjectives.

Word (adjective)	Definition	Negation	Definition (negated form)
aware	Conscious or informed about something.	un+aware	Not conscious of or informed about something.
common	Occurring frequently or shared by all.	un+common	Rare or not usual.
finished	Completed or ended.	un+finished	Not completed or ended.
deniable	Able to be denied or disputed.	un+deniable	Impossible to deny or dispute; clearly true.
founded	Established or based on.	un+founded	Not based on fact or reason.

Word (adjective)	Definition	Negation	Definition (negated form)
yielding	Producing or providing.	un+yielding	Not producing or yielding the expected amount.
sustainable	Able to be maintained at a certain rate or level.	un+sustainable	Not able to be maintained at a certain level or rate.
biased	Showing prejudice for or against someone or something.	un+biased	Without prejudice; fair or impartial.

Activity 4: Read each sentence carefully. Choose the correct form of the adjectives from the options provided (either the positive or negated form) to best complete the sentence. Fill in the blank with your chosen adjective. Pay attention to the context to determine which form is appropriate.

Aware	Common	Finished	Deniable
Yielding	Sustainable	Founded	Biased

1. She strove to remain _____ while judging the competition, treating all participants equally regardless of her personal preferences.

2. The community garden promoted _____ practices by encouraging the use of organic fertilizers and recycled water.

3. The artist declared the mural _____, stepping back to admire the vibrant colors that now adorned the old city wall.

4. She was completely _____ of the surprise party her friends were planning for her birthday.

5. Relying solely on fossil fuels is _____ in the long term due to their environmental impact and finite supply.

6. The rumors of the school closing were _____, as confirmed by the principal during the assembly.

7. The arguments in her essay were well-_____ on extensive research and clear logical reasoning.

8. It's a _____ misconception that you can see the Great Wall of China from space, but this is not true.

9. It's _____ to find a blue lobster in nature because the genetic mutation that causes the color is very rare.

10. His talent for solving complex mathematical problems quickly was _____, impressing both his teachers and peers.

11. The _____ land failed to produce a viable crop this season, leaving the farmers concerned about future yields.

12. The sculpture stood _____ in the studio, waiting for the artist to add the final touches.

13. The news report was criticized for being _____, presenting only one side of the controversial story.

14. The evidence against the suspect was hardly _____, leading the jury to a quick verdict.

15. The fertile soil was _____, producing an abundant harvest that sustained the entire community.

LESSON 34: The Prefixes "im-," "ir-," "il-," "in-"

 As we learned in the previous lesson, a prefix can dramatically shift the meaning of a word to its opposite. In this lesson, we will broaden our exploration to include other powerful prefixes such as "im-," "ir-," "il-," and "in-." Like "un-," these prefixes transform words into their opposites, making them very useful for expressing negation or contradiction.

Negation prefixes are fascinating because they help us express what something is not, rather than what it is. For instance:

- "Im-" before "possible" gives us "impossible," indicating something that cannot be done.
- "Ir-" in front of "regular" transforms it into "irregular," which means not following the usual rules or patterns.
- "Il-" attached to "logical" becomes "illogical," meaning something that does not make sense.
- "In-" added to "dependent" results in "independent," describing someone who does not rely on others.

Like the tools in a painter's kit, each of these prefixes helps us paint clearer pictures with our words, allowing us to articulate more complex ideas and emotions.

You might wonder why English has such a variety of prefixes that all seem to serve the same purpose. The answer lies in the diverse languages that have influenced English throughout its history. The prefixes "im-," "in-," "ir-," and "il-" all originate from Latin, where they were used to negate words. However, the specific prefix used often depends on the letter that follows it.

Guidelines: The Prefix "im-"

- The prefix "im-" is commonly used in English to negate the meanings of adjectives, particularly those that begin with "p" or "m." It transforms the base words into their opposites, emphasizing the negation or lack of the original trait.

Activity 1: Review and study the provided tables to understand how the prefixes listed alter the meanings of the words.

Base Word (adjective)	Definition	Negation (im-)	Definition (negated form)
mature	Showing adult behavior.	im+mature	Behaving in a childish way.
mortal	Able to die.	im+mortal	Not subject to death or living forever.

Base Word (adjective)	Definition	Negation (im-)	Definition (negated form)
mobile	Able to move or be moved freely and easily.	im+mobile	Unable to move or be moved.
mutable	Able to change or be changed	im+mutable	Unchanging over time or unable to be changed.
measurable	Capable of being measured	im+measurable	Too large, extensive, or extreme to measure.
perfect	Completely correct or accurate.	im+perfect	Having flaws or errors.
polite	Showing good manners and respect in behavior or speech.	im+polite	Not showing good manners.

Base Word (adjective)	Definition	Negation (im-)	Definition (negated form)
partial	Favoring one side in a dispute over another	im+partial	Fair and unbiased; not favoring one side over another.
permeable	Allowing liquids or gases to pass through it.	im+permeable	Not allowing fluid or gas to pass through.
practical	Useful and sensible, applied to real-world situations.	im+practical	Unrealistic or inefficient.
possible	Able to be done or achieved	im+possible	Not able to be done or achieved.

Activity 2: Read each sentence and select the correct word form from the provided options (either positive or negated) to complete the sentence. Fill in the blank with your choice, considering the context to determine the appropriate form.

Mature	Mutable	Polite
Measurable	Partial	Possible
Mobile	Perfect	Practical
Mortal	Permeable	

1. Despite his frustration, he remained _____ and thanked the customer service representative for their help.

2. The city's new gardening initiative used _____ paving materials that allowed rainwater to seep through and irrigate the plants.

3. It was _____ of him to interrupt the speaker with his loud comments.

4. With the advancements in technology, traveling to Mars might become _____ within our lifetime.

5. The new science exhibit featured a _____ planetarium that could be transported to schools across the county.

6. The handcrafted vase was beautiful, even though it was slightly _____.

7. The success of the fundraising event was _____ by the significant increase in donations compared to last year.

8. The workshop taught us _____ skills, like how to change a tire and check the oil level in a car.

8. The workshop taught us _____ skills, like how to change a tire and check the oil level in a car.

9. The judge declared a mistrial due to a _____ jury that had been unduly influenced by media coverage

Mature	Mutable	Polite
Measurable	Partial	Possible
Mobile	Perfect	Practical
Mortal	Permeable	

10. Her decision was _____, despite her friends' attempts to convince her otherwise.

11. After the snowstorm, the abandoned cars were _____, buried under feet of snow.

12. She practiced every evening until her performance was _____, not missing a single note.

13. His opinions on the matter were _____, changing subtly with each new article he read.

14. In ancient myths, gods often mingled with _____ beings, influencing their fates and the course of human history.

15. Jason's _____ behavior at the assembly led to a stern warning from the principal.

16. The influence of her kind gesture was _____, spreading joy throughout the community.

17. Legends say that the fountain of youth grants _____ life to all who drink from its waters.

18. Although only a freshman, Jenna handled the criticism with a _____ perspective that impressed her older peers.

19. Wearing high heels on a hiking trip proved _____ and soon turned uncomfortable.

20. The mediator remained _____, treating both parties in the dispute with equal fairness.

21. The laboratory gloves were made of an _____ material that prevented chemicals from passing through.

22. Climbing the sheer cliff without equipment seemed _____, but the experienced climber was determined.

Guidelines: The Prefix "ir-"

- The prefix "ir-" is used to form the negatives of adjectives, conveying the sense of "not" or "the opposite of." It is generally added to adjectives beginning with the letter "r" to create their antonyms. This usage helps maintain pronunciation ease and clarity, as placing "ir-" before other letters might result in awkward or unclear pronunciation.

Activity 3: Review and study the provided table to understand how the prefix "ir-" alters the meanings of the words.

Base Word (adjective)	Definition	Negation (ir-)	Definition (negated form)
rational	Logical and reasonable.	ir-rational	Not logical or reasonable.
regular	Occurring at fixed intervals; consistent in pattern.	ir-regular	Occurring at unpredictable intervals; not following a pattern.

Base Word (adjective)	Definition	Negation (ir-)	Definition (negated form)
relevant	Closely connected or appropriate to the matter at hand.	ir+relevant	Not related to or pertinent to the matter at hand.
responsible	Accountable for something within one's power, control, or management.	ir+responsible	Not accountable for one's actions or duties; lacking a sense of responsibility.
reversible	Capable of being turned or flipped to the opposite state.	ir+reversible	Not able to be turned back to a previous state.
recoverable	Able to be regained or restored.	ir+recoverable	Not able to be regained or restored.
reproachable	Deserving criticism or censure.	ir+reproachable	Beyond criticism; faultless.

Base Word (adjective)	Definition	Negation (ir-)	Definition (negated form)
resolvable	Capable of being solved or settled.	ir-resolvable	Impossible to solve or settle.
refutable	Able to be proven wrong or false.	ir-refutable	Impossible to disprove or deny.

Activity 4: Read each sentence in the "Positive Sentence" column carefully. In the "Negation" column, write the opposite meaning of the bolded word by adding the appropriate prefix to the given word.

Positive Sentence	Negation
1. The data from the damaged hard drive was surprisingly **recoverable**, allowing the scientists to continue their research without much delay.	Had the data been severely damaged in the hard drive, it would have been _____.
2. The coach's behavior during the game was considered **reproachable**, and he faced disciplinary action for his conduct.	If the coach's behavior had been beyond criticism, it would have been _____.

Positive Sentence	Negation
3. As the team leader, she felt **responsible** for ensuring that everyone completed their tasks on time.	If she hadn't felt responsible, her attitude could have been described as _____.
4. The teacher emphasized the importance of maintaining a **regular** study schedule to improve grades.	If the study schedule had not been regular, it would have been _____.
5. The decision to cut down the ancient tree was **reversible**, as the town council could still choose to protect it.	Once the tree was cut down, the decision was _____.
6. The historian's findings were particularly **relevant** to understanding the ancient civilization's culture.	If the findings were not relevant, they would have been _____.
7. In a heated debate, it's crucial to present **rational** arguments rather than emotional outbursts.	When arguments are not rational, they are often _____.
8. The theory proposed by the young scientist was **refutable**, as it lacked sufficient evidence and had several flaws.	A theory that cannot be disproven is _____.
9. The conflict between the two friends seemed easily **resolvable** with a bit of honest communication.	When conflicts cannot be resolved, they are considered _____.

Guidelines: The Prefix "il-"

- The prefix "il-" is used to negate the meanings of adjectives and occasionally nouns. It is specifically used before words that start with the letter "l" to form their antonyms or express negation, enhancing pronunciation and clarity due to phonetic compatibility.

Activity 5: Review and study the provided tables to understand how the prefixes listed alter the meanings of the words.

Base Word (adjective)	Definition	Negation (il-)	Definition (negated form)
legal	Permitted by law.	il+legal	Not permitted by law.
legible	Clear enough to be read easily.	il+legible	Not clear enough to be read.

Base Word (adjective)	Definition	Negation (il-)	Definition (negated form)
legitimate	Authorized by law or accepted standards.	il+legitimate	Not authorized by law or accepted standards.
logical	Based on clear and sound reasoning.	il+logical	Not making sense or being reasonable.
literate	Able to read and write.	il+literate	Unable to read or write.
liberal	Open to new ideas or ways of behaving that differ from traditional norms.	il+liberal	Not open to new ideas or ways of behaving that differ from traditional norms.
luminous	Shining or bright.	il+luminous	Not bright or shining; dull.

Activity 6: Read each sentence in the "Positive Sentence" column carefully. In the "Negation" column, write the opposite meaning of the bolded word by adding the appropriate prefix to the given word.

Positive Sentence	Negation
1. His actions seemed completely **logical** under the circumstances.	If his actions hadn't been logical, they would have been _____.
2. The night sky was beautifully **luminous**, filled with countless stars.	If the night sky hadn't been luminous, it would have been _____.
3. The contract was **legitimate** and followed all legal requirements.	If the contract hadn't been legitimate, it would have been _____.
4. The university was known for its **liberal** policies that encouraged free speech.	If the university prohibited free speech, it would be an _____ university.
5. He was fully **literate**, able to read and write fluently.	If he didn't know how to read and write, he would be _____.
6. The handwriting was clear and **legible**, easy to read.	If the handwriting had been messy, it would have been _____.
7. Drinking alcohol is only **legal** for individuals over the age of 21 in many countries.	Drinking alcohol under the age of 21 is _____.

Guidelines: The Prefix "in-"

- The prefix "in-" is primarily used to negate the meanings of adjectives, effectively turning them into their opposites. It is occasionally used with some verbs and nouns as well. This prefix is commonly added to words starting with various letters.

Activity 7: Review and study the provided table to understand how the prefix "in-" alters the meanings of the words.

Base Word (adjective)	Definition	Negation (in-)	Definition (negated form)
active	Engaging in physical or mental activities.	in+active	Not engaging in or involving any or much physical activity.
correct	Right or accurate.	in+correct	Wrong.

Base Word (adjective)	Definition	Negation (in-)	Definition (negated form)
direct	Arising or occurring as a primary consequence or effect; straightforward.	in+direct	Arising or occurring as a secondary consequence or effect, not as a primary cause; not straightforward.
dependent	Relying on someone or something else for support.	in+dependent	Free from outside control
decent	Conforming to standards of propriety, good taste, or morality.	in+decent	Not conforming with generally accepted standards of behavior.
definite	Clearly stated or decided; not vague or doubtful.	in+definite	Lasting for an unknown length of time.

Base Word (adjective)	Definition	Negation (in-)	Definition (negated form)
flexible	Able to bend easily without breaking; adaptable to change.	in+flexible	Stiff or rigid; unwilling to change or compromise.
tolerant	Accepting of differences in others, such as beliefs or behaviors.	in+tolerant	Unwilling to accept or respect differing opinions, beliefs, or behaviors.
visible	Able to be seen; not hidden from view.	in+visible	Not able to be seen.
flexible	Able to bend easily without breaking; adaptable to change.	in+flexible	Stiff or rigid; unwilling to change or compromise.
tolerant	Accepting of differences in others, such as beliefs or behaviors.	in+tolerant	Unwilling to accept or respect differing opinions, beliefs, or behaviors.
visible	Able to be seen; not hidden from view.	in+visible	Not able to be seen.

Base Word	Definition	Negation (in-)	Definition (negated form)
validate (verb)	To confirm or prove the correctness of something.	in+validate	To make something no longer valid or acceptable.
justice (noun)	The fair and moral treatment according to the law or ethical standards.	in+justice	The lack of fairness or violation of the rights of others.
ability (noun)	The skill or means to do something.	in+ability	The lack of skill, means, or capability to do something.

 Activity 8: Fill in the blanks with the correct form of the word. For each sentence pair, one uses the positive form and the other the negated form with "in-." Use the context of the sentences to identify the correct word.

Active - Inactive:

1. After the eruption in 79 AD that buried Pompeii, Mount Vesuvius remained _____ for nearly three centuries before erupting again in 472 AD.

2. The volcano in Hawaii was very _____ during the early 20th century, with frequent eruptions.

Correct - Incorrect:

3. His answer was _____ because he didn't apply the Pythagorean theorem properly.

4. Marie Curie's _____ identification of radium and polonium as new elements significantly advanced the study of radioactivity.

Direct - Indirect:

5. The most _____ route from New York to Los Angeles is by flying.

6. The Cold War had an _____ impact on technological advancements, as the competition between the United States and the Soviet Union spurred innovation in various fields including space exploration and military technology.

Dependent - Independent:

7. Many retirees are _____ on Social Security benefits as a primary source of income during their retirement years.

8. India became an _____ nation on August 15, 1947, following nearly 200 years of British colonial rule.

Decent - Indecent:

9. During the 1984 U.S. presidential campaign, Ronald Reagan's comment about bombing Russia during a sound test was considered _____ and caused a significant public outcry.

10. In his book "A Theory of Justice," philosopher John Rawls argued that a _____ society is one that ensures fair opportunities and respects the rights of all its citizens.

Flexible - Inflexible:

11. Gymnasts need to be extremely _____ to perform their routines.

12. During World War II, General Montgomery's _____ strategies often led to disagreements with his more adaptable counterparts.

Tolerant - Intolerant:

13. During the Spanish Inquisition, authorities were _____ of any religious beliefs that deviated from Catholicism, leading to widespread persecution.

14. The community is known for being _____ of different cultures and traditions.

Visible - Invisible:

15. The satellite images provided _____ proof of the rapidly forming hurricane, allowing meteorologists to issue timely warnings to affected areas.

16. In chemistry, the presence of certain gases, such as carbon monoxide, is _____ to the naked eye but can be detected using specialized sensors and indicators.

Validate - Invalidate:

17. The introduction of the theory of relativity by Albert Einstein helped _____ the long-standing Newtonian concepts of absolute time and space, revolutionizing our understanding of physics.

18. The discovery of the Rosetta Stone helped _____ the translation of Egyptian hieroglyphs, significantly advancing the field of Egyptology.

Justice - Injustice:

19. The internment of Japanese Americans during World War II is widely regarded as a grave _____, as thousands of innocent people were forcibly relocated and confined in camps solely based on their ethnicity.

20. The Civil Rights Act of 1964 was a landmark legislation in the United States, aimed at ensuring _____ by outlawing discrimination based on race, color, religion, sex, or national origin.

Ability - Inability:

21. Dolphins have the remarkable _____ to use echolocation to navigate and hunt for prey in murky waters.

22. In the early days of automobile development, inventors like Karl Benz faced numerous challenges due to the _____ of existing materials to withstand the high temperatures and pressures of internal combustion engines.

The prefix "in-" does not always create the antonym of the base word. In some cases, words start with the prefix "in-" to indicate "inside," "within," "toward" or "addition". This usage is inherited from Latin and applies to many words of Latin origin. Study the table below, which shows what the prefix "in-" indicates. The definition of each word is provided based on its original Latin meaning. You will notice that some words have retained a meaning similar to their original Latin definition, while others have evolved to have more specific definitions.

Activity 9: Review and study the provided table.

Latin Root Word	Latin Origin Indication and Definition	Definition in Modern Usage
Increase	Indication: **Addition**. Definition: To grow in size.	To make or become larger in size, amount, or number.
Indigenous	Indication: **Within**. Definition: Born within a place.	Originating naturally in a particular place; native.
Industrious	Indication: **Within**. Definition: To work diligently within a task.	Hardworking and diligent.

Latin Root Word	Latin Origin Indication and Definition	Definition in Modern Usage
Invite	Indication: **Toward**. Definition: To call toward.	To ask someone to attend or participate.
Intense	Indication: **Within**. Definition: Tightly within.	Strong or extreme in degree.
Interior	Indication: **Within**. Definition: Inside or inner.	The inside part of something.
Involve	Indication: **Within**. Definition: To wrap up within.	To include as a necessary part or result.
Intricate	Indication: **Within**. Definition: Entangled within.	Very detailed and complex.
Include	Indication: **Addition**. Definition: To comprise as part of a whole.	To comprise as part of a whole.

Latin Root Word	Latin Origin Indication and Definition	Definition in Modern Usage
Incorporate	Indication: **Addition**. Definition: To include as part of a whole.	To combine or unite into one body.
Inform	Indication: **Within**. Definition: To form within.	To give knowledge or information to.

While it is not always easy to identify whether a word starting with "in-" is negating or modifying the base word in other ways, there are some guidelines that can help you decide if the prefixed word indicates the opposite of the base word or if it means "within," "toward," or "addition." Here are some guidelines and tips to help you decipher words beginning with the prefix "in-." Remember, however, that these are not absolute rules and there will always be exceptions.

1. Identify the Base Word:
Understanding the base word can help you determine if the prefix "in-" indicates negation or not.

Examples:
a) The base word in "invisible" is "visible," which means "able to be seen." Here, "in-" indicates negation.

b) The base word of "involve" is "volve." This word does not stand on its own in the English language but has its root in Latin. This indicates that the prefix "in-" functions as inclusion, not negation.

c) The base word of "inform" is "form," which originates from Latin, meaning "shape." This indicates inclusion and not negation because it means "to give shape to the knowledge you have within" or "to provide knowledge."

d) The base word of "increase" is "crease" which does not stand on its own in the English language and has its origin in Latin. In this case, "in-" indicates "addition."

2. Use Context Clues:
Use the sentence within which the word is used to help you determine its meaning. The sentence it is contained in often suggests whether it is a negation, inclusion or addition.

Examples:

a) Sentence:
The teacher was **intolerant** of any form of disrespect in the classroom, enforcing strict rules to maintain order.

Explanation:
The sentence talks about the teacher enforcing strict rules to maintain order and not accepting disrespect. This suggests that the teacher is "not willing to accept" disrespect. From this context, you can tell that "in-" is used for negation, making the word mean the opposite of "tolerant."

b) Sentence:
The artist spent months creating an **intricate** design, with each tiny detail carefully refined to perfection.

Explanation:
In this sentence, the context tells you that the design is very detailed and complex. Since the sentence emphasizes the many details included within the design, you can decipher that "in-" here indicates inclusion or being "within."

c) Sentence:
The new curriculum will **incorporate** more hands-on activities to enhance student engagement and learning.

Explanation:
The sentence mentions a new curriculum with hands-on activities that will enhance or improve engagement and learning. This suggests that "incorporate" means to include or add these activities into the curriculum. From this context, you can tell that "in-" signifies inclusion or addition, meaning to bring something into the whole.

3. Dictionary Use
When in doubt, use a dictionary to verify the meaning and see if "in-" serves as a negation or another function. A dictionary is a valuable tool for understanding the prefix "in-." When you look up a word, the definition and usage examples help determine if "in-" indicates negation, inclusion, addition, or direction. Many dictionaries also include an etymology

section (word origin), which provides the word's origin and historical development. This etymological information clarifies how the prefix functions in different contexts. By comparing the base word and the prefixed word, and reviewing their meanings, you can accurately understand the role of "in-" in forming the word. For example, Merriam-Webster's online dictionary has a section titled "Word History" where you can verify the word's origin and the function of prefixes. Here's an example of how this would look for the word "inflate":

Word History
Etymology
Middle English, from Latin *inflatus*, past participle of *inflare*, from *in-* + *flare* to blow

Activity 10: Decide whether the "in-" in the bolded word in each sentence indicates negation (N), inclusion (I), addition (A), or direction (D).

Sentence	Negation (N), Inclusion (I), Addition (A), Direction (D)
1. The **industrious** student spent every evening studying and completing homework assignments.	
2. Since she moved out of her parents' house, Jody has become much more **independent**, making her own decisions and managing her own finances.	
3. Many different species of animals **inhabit** the dense rainforest.	

Sentence	Negation (N), Inclusion (I), Addition (A), Direction (D)
4. The nurse will **inject** the medicine directly into the patient's vein.	
5. The discovery of new evidence will **invalidate** the previous conclusion, showing it to be incorrect.	
6. The protesters marched through the city to speak out against the **injustice** they felt was happening in their community.	
7. The new manager was **inflexible**, refusing to change his plans even when it was clear they weren't working.	
8. To prepare for the party, we need to **inflate** all the balloons until they are fully blown up.	
9. Before handing in your essay, be sure to **inspect** it closely for any errors or mistakes.	

LESSON 35: The Prefixes "dis-," "mis-,""anti-," "non-"

The final four prefixes we'll be exploring in this part of the book are "dis-," "mis-,""anti-" and "non-." Did you know that each of these prefixes has a character of its own?

"Dis-" is "The Opposer," like a superhero's enemy. It opposes or reverses the meaning of a word right at the very beginning. **"Mis-,"** on the other hand, is **"The Mistake Maker."** It is the trickster prefix that often signals something has gone wrong or a mistake has been made. **"Anti-"** is **"The Great Opponent,"** always standing against something and offering resistance. Finally, **"non-"** is **"The Absence Indicator,"** the prefix that always signifies the absence or lack of something.

Let's explore each of these prefixes further.

The Prefix "dis-"

The prefix "dis-" is commonly used to form words that indicate **negation**, **opposition**, or **reversal**. Here are some guidelines to help you understand how to use "dis-" effectively:

1. Negation or Absence:

Examples:
- **Disagree: To not agree.**
- **Dislike: To not like.**

2. Reversal of Action:

Examples:
- **Disconnect: To undo the connection.**
- **Disarm: To remove weapons from someone.**

3. Opposition:

Examples:
Disapprove: To express an opinion against something.
Disbelieve: To not believe.

4. Usage with Verbs:

Examples:
- **Discontinue:** To stop doing something.
- **Disinherit:** To deprive someone of an inheritance.

5. Usage with Adjectives: "Dis-" can also be added to adjectives to form their negative counterparts.

Examples:
- **Discontent:** Not content or satisfied.
- **Disorganized:** Not organized.

6. Common Patterns: "Dis-" is typically followed by a base word that can be easily recognized. Understanding the base word helps in predicting the meaning.

Examples:
- **Disrespect:** Opposite of respect.
- **Disappear:** Opposite of appear.

Activity 1: Decide what each of the bolded words with the prefix "dis-" means within the context of the sentence. Pay close attention to the to the base word and the context in which it is used, as this will help you accurately identify its definition.

1. Growing up in a remote village can be a significant **disadvantage** when it comes to accessing quality education.
The word "**disadvantage**" in this sentence means _____

_____

2. The researchers needed to **disaggregate** the data to better understand the individual contributions to the overall results.
The word "**disaggregate**" in this sentence means _____

_____

3. Her parents **disapprove** of her decision to drop out of college to pursue a career in music.

The word "**disapprove**" in this sentence means _____

_____

4. The treaty called for the **disarmament** of all nuclear weapons to ensure global peace and security.

The word "**disarmament**" in this sentence means _____

_____

5. After the hurricane, the entire town was in **disarray**, with debris scattered everywhere.

The word "**disarray**" in this sentence means _____

_____

6. Before moving to their new house, they had to **disassemble** the furniture to fit it through the doorways.

The word "**disassemble**" in this sentence means _____

_____

7. She felt a sharp **discomfort** in her stomach after eating the spicy meal.

The word "**discomfort**" in this sentence means _____

_____

8. The unexpected question from the reporter seemed to **disconcert** the politician, causing him to hesitate.

The word "**disconcert**" in this sentence means _____

_____

9. The workers expressed their **discontent** with the new policies by organizing a strike.

The word "**discontent**" in this sentence means _____

_____

10. Due to safety concerns, the company decided to **discontinue** the production of the faulty product.

The word "**discontinue**" in this sentence means _____

_____

11. The accountant noticed a **discrepancy** between the company's financial statements and the bank records.

The word "**discrepancy**" in this sentence means _____

_____

12. The new law was criticized because it could **disenfranchise** many eligible voters by making it harder to register.

The word "**disenfranchise**" in this sentence means _____

_____

13. The lack of progress on their project began to **dishearten** the team.

The word "**disconcert**" in this sentence means _____

_____

14. The billionaire threatened to **disinherit** his son if he didn't change his irresponsible behavior.

The word "**disinherit**" in this sentence means _____

_____

The Prefix "mis-"

The prefix "mis-" is used to indicate **something done incorrectly, wrongly, or badly.** Here are some guidelines to help you understand how to use "mis-" effectively:

1. Indicating Errors or Mistakes: "Mis-" is commonly used to show that an action is performed incorrectly or that an error has occurred.

Examples:
- **Misunderstand: To understand wrongly.**
- **Misinterpret: To interpret wrongly.**

2. Signifying Wrong Actions or Behavior: Use "mis-" to describe actions or behavior that are inappropriate or incorrect.

Examples:
- **Misbehave: To behave badly.**
- **Mislead: To lead in the wrong direction.**

3. Incorrect Usage or Application: "Mis-" can indicate that something is used or applied incorrectly.

Examples:
- **Misuse: To use something wrongly.**
- **Misinform: To give false or incorrect information.**

4. Expressing Failure or Deficiency: "Mis-" can also denote failure or lack in performing an action or achieving a result.

Examples:
- **Misfire: To fail to fire or work correctly.**
- **Misplace: To put something in the wrong place.**

Activity 2: Below are sentences with missing words that have the prefix "mis-." Use the word bank to fill in the blanks. This activity will help you understand how "mis-" words indicate (a) errors or mistakes, (b) wrong actions or behavior, (c) incorrect usage or application, or (d) failure or deficiency. From the context of each sentence, determine which category the missing word belongs to and choose the best word to complete the sentence.

Errors or Mistakes	Wrong Action or Behavior	Wrong Usage or Application	Failure or Deficiency
Misquote	Misuse	Miscalculate	Misfire
Miscalculate	Misbehave	Misuse	Misdiagnose
Misspell	Mistreat	Misapply	Mismanage
Misinterpret	Mislead	Misinterpret	Misplace
Misprint	Misdirect	Misquote	Misunderstand

1. He tried to _____ his parents about his grades, but they found out the truth.

2. The student was penalized for _____ the school's computer for personal games.

3. She was warned not to _____ the lab equipment, as it could be dangerous.

4. The prankster _____ the delivery driver to the wrong address.

5. Don't _____ the data; make sure you understand what it really means.

6. It's easy to _____ complex instructions, so ask questions if you're unsure.

7. It is cruel to _____ animals, and there are laws to protect them from harm.

8. The newspaper had a _____ on the front page, listing the wrong date for the event.

9. The students were told not to _____ during the assembly to avoid disrupting the event.

10. If you _____ the recipe ingredients, the cake won't turn out right.

11. It's easy to _____ words when you're writing quickly, so always double-check your spelling.

12. He _____ the total cost of the project, leading to a budget shortfall.

13. She _____ the teacher's instructions and did the wrong assignment.

14. The article _____ the scientist, causing confusion about the research findings.

15. The plan to surprise her friend seemed to _____, as her friend already knew about it.

16. Be careful not to _____ your sources when writing your research paper.

17. The project was delayed because the team leader _____ the resources.

18. If you _____ the formula, the math problem will be solved incorrectly.

19. He tends to _____ his keys frequently, causing him to be late.

20. The doctor apologized for having _____ the condition.

The Prefix "anti-"

The prefix "anti-" is commonly used to form words that mean **"against," "opposite of,"** or **"preventing."** Here are some guidelines:

Meaning: "Anti-" indicates opposition, prevention, or reversal. For example, "antibiotic" means against life (germs).

Hyphenation: Generally, "anti-" is not hyphenated unless it precedes a proper noun (e.g., anti-American) or if the hyphen avoids double "i" (e.g., anti-inflammatory).

Formation: Combine "anti-" with nouns or adjectives to form words like "antifreeze" (against freezing) or "antivirus" (against viruses).

The Prefix "non-"

The prefix "non-" is used to form words that mean **"not"** or **"without."** Here are some guidelines:

Meaning: "Non-" indicates absence, negation, or exclusion. For example, "nonsense" means without sense.

Hyphenation: Generally, "non-" is not hyphenated unless it precedes a proper noun (e.g., non-European) or when the base word is already hyphenated (e.g., non-profit-making).

Formation: Combine "non-" with nouns, adjectives, or verbs to create words like "nonstop" (without stopping) or "nondairy" (without dairy).

Activity 3: Review and study the provided table to understand the differences between the prefixes "anti-" and "non-."

	Anti-	**Non-**
Usage	Use when describing something that opposes or counteracts another thing.	Use when describing something that lacks a particular feature or does not involve something.
Examples	• Antibiotic (against bacteria) • Antisocial (opposes social behavior) • Antifreeze (against freezing) • Antiwar (opposed to war) • Antibacterial (preventing the growth of bacteria)	• Nonfiction (not fiction) • Nonresident (not a resident) • Nonstop • Nonsmoker (someone who does not smoke) • Nonprofit (does not make profit)

Activity 4: Fill in the blanks with the appropriate "anti-" or "non-" word from the word bank. Each word fits into one of the sentences below. Use the context of the sentence to help you choose the correct word.

antagonist	antifungal	nonconformist	nonnegotiable
antibody	antioxidant	nonessential	nonstop
anticorrosive	antithesis	nonexistent	nontoxic
antidote	noncompetitive	nonfiction	nonviolent

1. In cases of snake bites, an _____ made from antivenom can neutralize the venom and save the victim's life.

2. Before the discovery of penicillin, effective treatments for bacterial infections were virtually _____.

3. In the novel "Harry Potter and the Philosopher's Stone," Lord Voldemort serves as the primary _____, opposing Harry throughout the series.

4. "The Diary of Anne Frank" is a _____ book that gives a firsthand account of a Jewish girl's life during the Holocaust.

5. Ships' hulls are often coated with _____ paint to prevent rust and damage from prolonged exposure to seawater.

6. Crayola crayons are made from _____ materials, making them safe for children to use.

7. Blueberries are known for their high levels of _____, which help protect the body against free radicals and oxidative stress.

8. The Cold War era was marked by the _____ of the capitalist United States and the communist Soviet Union, each promoting opposing ideologies.

9. The Special Olympics offers _____ events where athletes of all abilities can participate and showcase their skills.

10. In the 1960s, the Beatles were seen as _____ who challenged traditional norms and revolutionized popular music.

antagonist	antifungal	nonconformist	nonnegotiable
antibody	antioxidant	nonessential	nonstop
anticorrosive	antithesis	nonexistent	nontoxic
antidote	noncompetitive	nonfiction	nonviolent

11. During the COVID-19 pandemic, scientists developed vaccines that help the body produce _____ to fight the virus.

12. Athletes often use _____ creams to treat conditions like athlete's foot, which is caused by fungal infections.

13. In 1927, Charles Lindbergh made the first _____ solo transatlantic flight from New York to Paris.

14. Mahatma Gandhi led India to independence through _____ resistance, inspiring civil rights movements around the world.

15. The abolition of slavery was a _____ demand for the Union during the American Civil War.

16. During the COVID-19 pandemic, governments around the world closed _____ businesses to slow the spread of the virus.

LESSON 36: Suffixes

What are Suffixes?

You can think of suffixes as little word-ending sprinkles that add flavor and flair to your words. Suffixes are letters or groups of letters added to the end of a base word. These tiny endings can change the meaning of a word, tell us what part of speech it is, or even show us tense and number.

Imagine your base word is a plain cupcake. Adding a suffix is like adding frosting and decorations to turn that cupcake into a delicious masterpiece! Here are a few things suffixes can do:

- **Change Meaning**: Turn a noun into an adjective, like "joy" into "joy**ful**."
- **Indicate Tense**: Show when something happened, like "walk" into "walk**ed**."
- **Form Plurals**: Make words mean more than one, like "suffix" into "suffix**es**."
- **Show Comparisons**: Compare things, like "large" into "larg**er**" or "larg**est**".

Why are Suffixes Useful?

Suffixes are super useful because they help us express ourselves more clearly and precisely. For instance, do you want to describe something full of beauty? Add "-ful" to "beauty" and you've got "beautiful."

Do you need to talk about something that can be done? Add "-able" to "enjoy" and now you have "enjoyable." What about describing something lacking something? Add "-less" to "hope" and you get "hopeless." And don't forget the suffix "-ible," which turns "flex" into "flexible" to describe something that can bend easily. With these suffixes, you can create new words and ideas, making your speech and writing more colorful and dynamic!

Now that you know why suffixes are so useful, get ready to dive deeper! The upcoming lessons will focus on the suffixes "-ful," "-less," "-able," and "-ible." Rules and guidelines for each of these suffixes will be provided, helping you understand how to use them to transform and enhance your words.

LESSON 37: The Suffix "-ful"

 When we want to say that something is full of something else, or that something is abundant or consistently done, we use "-ful" at the end of the word to express such fullness. However, notice that the last "l" in "full" is dropped when it is used as a suffix. For example:

- If you want to say that a painting is full of color, you say, "The painting is very color**ful**."

- If you want to say that there was a lot of food at the party, you can use the word "bounti**ful**," which means "abundant."

- If you want to say that your dog is always playing, you say, "My dog is very play**ful**."

- If you want to say that your grandma gave you a huge plate of food, you would describe it as a "plate**ful**."

Do you notice that in each of these words, **"full" drops the final "l"?**

When adding the suffix "-ful" to a base word, the final "l" in "full" is omitted. This rule is straightforward, as the final "l" is dropped in nearly all words that incorporate the suffix "-ful."

Note: There are virtually NO words in English that end with "-full."

Words ending in "y"

When adding the suffix "-ful" to words ending in "y," it's important to look at the letter before the "y." If the letter is a consonant, the "y" changes to "i." If the letter is a vowel, the "y" stays the same. For example:

- In the word "duty," the "y" follows a consonant ("t"), so it becomes "dutiful."
- In the word "play," the "y" follows a vowel ("a"), so it remains "playful."

Notice that "duty" becomes "dutiful," with the "y" changing to "i," while "play" becomes "playful," keeping the "y."

Activity 1: Let's practice adding the suffix "-ful" to words. This exercise will help you become familiar with the suffix and its spelling. Complete each sentence by adding the suffix "-ful" to the base word in parentheses.

1. The kitten was _____ (play) and entertained everyone in the room.

2. Her _____ (beauty) smile lit up the entire room.

3. We had a _____ (wonder) time at the amusement park.

4. The _____ (joy) news made everyone happy.

5. The sky was clear and _____ (peace).

6. She received a _____ (thought) gift from her friend.

7. The _____ (grace) dancer moved effortlessly across the stage.

8. The teacher gave a _____ (help) explanation that cleared up all the confusion.

9. His _____ (care) approach prevented any accidents.

10. The _____ (plenty) harvest provided food for the entire village.

11. Her _____ (mercy) nature made her a beloved leader.

12. In the face of adversity, she proved to be incredibly _____ (resource), finding innovative solutions to problems that stumped everyone else.

13. His _____ (spite) remarks hurt everyone's feelings.

14. The _____ (vengeance) act led to a long-standing feud.

15. Despite the awful weather, she remained _____ (cheer) and optimistic.

16. The student's _____ (respect) attitude towards teachers earned him high praise.

17. She felt _____ (grate) for all the help she received during the difficult times.

18. The _____ (event) party had surprises at every turn.

19. Despite his charming demeanor, his _____ (deceit) actions soon revealed his true nature, leaving her feeling betrayed.

20. After realizing the impact of his harsh words, he felt deeply _____ (remorse) and sought to make amends with those he had hurt.

21. The old man's eyes were _____ (sorrow) as he reminisced about the friends he had lost over the years.

22. The _____ (mourn) melody of the violin echoed through the empty hall, capturing the depth of her grief.

LESSON 38: The Suffix "-less"

 When we want to describe something as missing or lacking, the suffix "-less" is our go-to tool. By adding "-less" to a base word, we convey the idea of being "without" something. For example, if your superhero has no fear, you would call them "fearless." If the night sky is missing stars, you describe it as "starless." In essence, adding the suffix "-less" to a base word signifies that something is absent or lacking.

Using the suffix "-less" is easy because it is simply added to the base word. Note the following examples:

End + less = Endless
Use + less = Useless
Hope + less = Hopeless

Note: When adding the suffix "-less" to base words with a silent "e," such as "hope" and "use," the "e" is retained.

Words ending in "l"

There are a limited number of words ending in "l" that accept the suffix "-less." The most commonly used examples are as follows:

Skill + less = Skilless

It is important to note that retaining the double "l" from "skill" would result in a triple "l," which is not permissible in English spelling. Consequently, one "l" is omitted.

Tail + less = Tailless
Soul + less = Soulless

Words ending in "y"

Few words ending in "y" take the suffix "-less." When this occurs, the "y" changes to "i." The most frequently used words in this category include:

Pity + less = Pitiless
Mercy + less = Merciless
Penny + less = Penniless

✏️ **Activity 1: Fill in the blank by adding the suffix "-less" to the base word in parentheses, indicating the absence or lack of the quality described.**

1. Despite their tireless efforts, the team felt _____ (hope) as the deadline loomed closer without any significant progress.

2. The scientist's _____ (care) handling of the chemical substances led to a dangerous spill that could have been avoided.

3. The explorer was mesmerized by the seemingly _____ (end) expanse of the desert, where the dunes stretched out as far as the eye could see.

4. The city council implemented new initiatives to provide support and shelter for the growing _____ (home) population.

5. With a _____ (fear) determination, the young activist spoke out against injustice, inspiring others to join the cause.

6. The museum's newest exhibit featured a _____ (price) collection of artifacts from ancient civilizations.

7. His _____ (thought) remarks during the meeting offended several colleagues and created an awkward atmosphere.

8. The _____ (tire) efforts of the volunteers ensured that the community event was a resounding success, despite numerous obstacles.

9. The _____ (reck) driver weaved through traffic at high speeds, endangering not only his life but also the lives of others on the road.

10. When she received the unexpected award, she was rendered _____ (speech), unable to find the words to express her gratitude.

11. The old coins, once thought to be valuable, turned out to be counterfeit and therefore _____ (worth) to collectors.

12. Despite months of negotiation, the peace talks were ultimately _____ (fruit), leaving both sides frustrated and without resolution.

13. Wandering through the streets with an _____ (aim) expression, he seemed lost in thought, unsure of where to go next.

14. The deer stood _____ (motion) in the clearing, its eyes fixed on the distant noise that had disturbed the forest's peace.

15. After a _____ (sleep) night filled with worry, she finally decided to confront the issue head-on.

LESSON 39: The Suffixes "-able" and "-ible"

 It is time to explore the dynamic duo "-able" and "-ible." These two partners transform ordinary words into adjectives, telling us something can be done or has a certain quality.

Knowing when to use "-able" versus "-ible" can be challenging sometimes. But don't worry because there are some general guidelines that you can learn, to help you decide which suffix to use with a given word.

Why is it important?
Understanding the difference between "-able" and "-ible" helps you spell words correctly and use them confidently in your writing. It's like having the right ingredients for a recipe—get it right, and everything turns out perfectly!

Here are some helpful guidelines to determine whether to use "-able" or "-ible."

1. Base Words That Stand Alone:

- **If the base word can stand alone as a complete word, you usually add "-able."**

Examples:

"Enjoy" becomes "enjoyable" (since "enjoy" is a complete word).
"Like" becomes "likeable" (since "like" is a complete word).

2. Latin Roots and Words That Can't Stand Alone:

If the root word is derived from Latin and can't stand alone in English, you usually add "-ible."

Examples:

"Aud" (from Latin "audire," meaning "to hear") becomes "audible."
"Vis" (from Latin "videre," meaning "to see") becomes "visible."
"Leg" (from Latin "legere," meaning "to read") becomes "legible."
"Cred" (from Latin "credere," meaning "to believe") becomes "credible."
"Poss" (from Latin "posse," meaning "to be able") becomes "possible."

Think of "-able" as the friendly suffix that likes to hang out with root words that can stand on their own. Meanwhile, "-ible" is a bit more exclusive, sticking with roots from its Latin family.

Exceptions and Variations:

Although the guidelines provided in points 1 and 2 are generally helpful, there are many exceptions. Note the following words, which, despite being derived from Latin and able to stand alone, still use the suffix "-ible." Additionally, observe that some of these words, ending with a silent "e," drop the "e" when the suffix "-ible" is added.

Base Word (verb)	Latin Root Word	Definition	Suffix (turns the verb to an adjective)
access	accedere (to approach or come to)	to obtain or retrieve information or a resource	access**ible**
reverse	revertere (to turn back)	to move backward	revers**ible**
collapse	collabi (to fall together)	to fall down suddenly	collaps**ible**
sense	sentire (to feel or perceive)	to become aware of something	sens**ible** (having or showing good judgment)
flex	flectere (to bend)	to bend	flex**ible**

Note that some Latin-derived words, which <u>cannot</u> stand on their own, still use the suffix "-able." Additionally, note that the Latin suffix "-abilis" translates to "-able" in English and is retained in these instances.

Latin Root Word	Latin Definition	Suffix "-able"	English Definition
inevit- (inevit**abilis**)	unavoidable	**inevitable**	same as Latin
vi- (vi**abilis**)	capable of living or developing	**viable**	same as Latin
navig- (navig**abilis**)	able to be sailed upon or suitable for navigation	**navigable**	same as Latin
port- (port**abilis**)	able to be carried	**portable**	same as Latin
applic- (applic**abilis**)	can be used	**applicable**	same as Latin
cap- (cap**abilis**)	able to hold or do something	**capable**	same as Latin
toler- (toler**abilis**)	endurable or bearable	**tolerable**	same as Latin
dur- (dur**abilis**)	lasting	**durable**	same as Latin

Activity 1: Below, you will see pairs of words. Only one word in each pair is correct. Your task is to identify the correct word with the appropriate suffix. Write the correct word in each pair, in the column provided.

This exercise will help you visually familiarize yourself with the correct use of "-able" and "-ible" suffixes. Take your time to go over each pair and refer to the guidelines in this lesson.

"-able"	"-ible"	Correct Spelling
enjoyable	enjoyible	
likeable	likeible	
appealable	appealible	
distillable	distillible	
repealable	repealible	
draftable	draftible	
audable	audible	
possable	possible	

"-able"	"-ible"	Correct Spelling
visable	visible	
credable	credible	
legable	legible	
accessable	accessible	
reversable	reversible	
collapsable	collapsible	
sensable	sensible	
flexable	flexible	
inevitable	inevitible	
viable	viible	

"-able"	"-ible"	Correct Spelling
navigable	navigible	
portable	portible	
applicable	applicible	
capable	capible	
tolerable	tolerible	
durable	durible	

In the space provided below, write down the words you believe you need to practice further.

- **Some words derived from Latin change the ending "d" to "s."**

Base Word (verb)	Latin Root Word	Definition	Suffix (turns the verb to an adjective)
comprehend	comprehendere (to grasp or to understand)	to understand	comprehensible (capable of being understood)
defend	defendere (to protect)	to ward off or to protect	defensible (capable of being defended)
apprehend	apprehendere (to grasp or to arrest)	to arrest	apprehensible (capable of being grasped or arrested)

- **Not all Latin-derived words ending with "d" follow this pattern.**

Base Word (verb)	Latin Root Word	Definition	Suffix (turns the verb to an adjective)
suspend	suspendere (to hang up)	to temporarily stop, or to hang	suspendible
impound	imponere (to put in or place upon)	to seize and hold legally	impoundable

155

Activity 2: Choose the right word from the word bank and fill in the blank in the two sentences provided for each word.

This exercise will help reinforce your understanding and ensure you can correctly use "d" ending words with the suffix "-ible" or "-able."

Apprehensible	**Defensible**	**Comprehensible**
Impoundable	**Suspendible**	

1. The theory of relativity, proposed by Albert Einstein, became more _____ to the public after it was explained in simpler terms by science communicators.

2. In the experiment, the magnet demonstrated that iron filings are _____ in a magnetic field, showing the power of electromagnetic forces.

3. The scientist's hypothesis was _____ with ample evidence from controlled experiments, demonstrating a clear link between greenhouse gases and global warming.

4. The mysterious disappearance of Amelia Earhart remains barely _____, as no conclusive evidence has ever been found to explain her fate.

5. During the Prohibition era, any vehicle found transporting alcohol was _____ by law enforcement, leading to many covert operations by bootleggers.

6. The Declaration of Independence is written in a manner that is _____, even to readers in the modern era, due to its clear language and straightforward presentation of ideas.

7. According to environmental regulations, any vessel found discharging pollutants into the ocean is _____ to prevent further ecological damage.

8. The weight of the golden gate bridge is _____ by its enormous cables, which were engineered to support the structure and withstand the forces of nature.

9. The intricate patterns of the Mayan calendar are _____ to archaeologists who have dedicated years to studying this ancient civilization.

10. The Great Wall of China was built to create a _____ barrier against invading armies, showcasing the strategic military planning of ancient Chinese civilizations.

3. Changing the Ending of the Base Word:

- If the base word ends in a silent "e," we usually drop the "e" before adding "-able" or "-ible."

Examples "-able":

"Adore" becomes "adorable."   "Choose" becomes "choosable."

"Desire" becomes "desirable."   "Pause" becomes "pausable."

"Value" becomes "valuable."   "Excuse" becomes "excusable."

Examples "-ible":

"Sense" becomes "sensible."

"Reduce" becomes "reducible."

Exceptions:

- Note that the following words have a long "e" sound at the end. To preserve this sound when adding the suffix "-able," the double "e" is maintained.

  "Agree" becomes "agreeable."

  "Disagree" becomes "disagreeable."

  "Foresee" becomes "foreseeable."

- If the base word ends in "ce" or "ge," keep the final "e" to maintain the soft "c" or "g" sound.

Examples:

"Notice" becomes "noticeable."

"Manage" becomes "manageable."

"Change" becomes "changeable."

"Salvage" becomes "salvageable."

✏️ Activity 3: Refer to the examples in point 3 above and select the words whose spelling you need to practice. Pay attention to when the silent "e" is retained or dropped when adding the suffixes "-able" or "-ible."

----------------------------   ----------------------------   ----------------------------

----------------------------   ----------------------------   ----------------------------

----------------------------   ----------------------------   ----------------------------

----------------------------   ----------------------------   ----------------------------

4. Words ending in "ve"

- The suffix "-able" usually follows words ending in "ve," and the silent "e" is usually dropped.

Examples:

Achieve	⟶ Achievable	Receive	⟶ Receivable
Believe	⟶ Believable	Retrieve	⟶ Retrievable
Conceive	⟶ Conceivable	Solve	⟶ Solvable
		Move	⟶ Movable

Note: "Perceive" changes to "percep<u>t</u>ible." It is derived from the Latin word "percipere" which means "to become aware of something through the senses."

5. Words ending in "t":

- Many words that end in "t" can take either the suffix "-ible" or "-able." Most of these words have Latin origins. Those that use the suffix "-ible" have retained the Latin suffix "-ibilis" while the others have adopted the more commonly used English suffix "-able." Because there aren't clear-cut rules to determine which suffix to use, it's essential to learn the spelling of each word individually.

 **Activity 4:** Review and study the provided table that shows which words ending in "t" take the suffix "-ible" and which ones take the suffix "-able." Use the third column to write down any words you feel you need to practice.

A list of definitions can be found at the end of this lesson.

Base Word (Verb)	Appropriate Suffix	Practice Spelling
construct	construct**ible**	
contempt	contempt**ible**	
digest	digest**ible**	

Base Word (Verb)	Appropriate Suffix	Practice Spelling
corrupt	corrupt**ible**	
combust	combust**ible**	
convert	convert**ible**	
collect	collect**ible**	
prevent	prevent**able**	
accept	accept**able**	
adopt	adopt**able**	
adjust	adjust**able**	
adapt	adapt**able**	
prevent	prevent**able**	
predict	predict**able**	
detest	detest**able**	

Vocabulary Glossary

A

Appeal *(verb):* To make a serious or urgent request, typically to the public.

Accept: To agree to take or receive something.

Adapt: To change in order to fit a new situation or environment.

Adjust: To change something slightly to make it fit or function better.

Adopt: To take something as your own, like an idea or a child.

C

Collect: To gather things together, often as a hobby or for study.

Combust: To catch fire and burn.

Construct: To build or put together something.

Contempt: A strong feeling of disliking and having no respect for someone or something.

Convert: To change something into a different form or use.

Corrupt: To make something or someone dishonest or immoral.

D

Detest: To strongly dislike something or someone.

Digest: To break down food in the stomach so the body can use it.

P

Predict: To say what you think will happen in the future.

Prevent: To stop something from happening.

Part 6
Greek and Latin Roots

LESSON 40: Greek and Latin Roots

 The study of word origins is fascinating. It helps us understand how ancient languages, like Greek and Latin, have shaped the words we use every day.

What are Roots?

In the context of language, a "root" is the most basic part of a word, carrying the core meaning. Think of a root as the foundation upon which words are built. By adding prefixes and suffixes to these roots, we can create new words with related meanings. Roots often come from ancient languages like Greek and Latin, and they form the building blocks of many words in the English language and other languages.

The Connection to the English Language

Greek and Latin were the languages of scholars, scientists, and theologians for many centuries. As a result, many English words, especially in academic, scientific, and technical fields, have their origins in Greek and Latin. Understanding these roots helps us decipher the meanings of unfamiliar words and enhances our vocabulary.

Why is it Important to study Greek and Latin Root Words?

Learning Greek and Latin roots allows you to understand and use a broader range of words. For example, knowing that "bio" means life (from Greek) helps you understand words like "biology" (the study of life) and "biography" (a written account of someone's life). When you encounter new or complex words, recognizing familiar roots can help you infer their meanings, which is particularly useful in academic reading and standardized tests. Additionally, understanding roots can aid in spelling and pronunciation; for instance, knowing the root "scrib" or "script" (to write, from Latin) helps you spell and pronounce words like "describe," "manuscript," and "inscription" correctly.

Connections to Other Languages

Many modern languages, such as Spanish, French, and Italian, also have roots in Latin. Learning these roots can provide a foundation for studying other languages, making it easier to learn and understand them.

Activity 1: Study the images provided, which illustrate various Latin roots along with example words underneath each image. Pay close attention to the Latin root and how it forms the basis for the meaning of each example word. This exercise will help you understand the connection between Latin roots and their English derivatives.

Audi

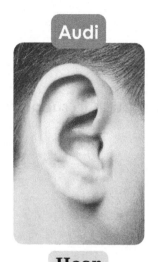

Hear

Audible
Auditorium
Audiobook

Dict

Speak

Dictate
Predict
Verdict

Junct

Join

Junction
Conjunction
Adjunct

Port

Carry

Portable
Import
Transport

Scrib, Script

Write

Describe
Manuscript
Prescription

Struct

Build

Construct
Instruct
Structure

Vis, Vid

See

Visible
Video
Visit

163

Activity 2: Read each sentence carefully. Identify the Latin root of the bold word and choose the best definition based on the context.

1. The teacher's voice was barely **audible** in the noisy classroom.

a) Visible
b) Able to be heard
c) Moveable
d) Understandable

2. The school held its annual concert in the large **auditorium**.

a) A place for meetings
b) A classroom
c) A dining hall
d) A theater

3. The jury reached a **verdict** after several hours of deliberation.

a) A decision
b) An argument
c) A discussion
d) A conclusion

4. The king issued an **edict** that all citizens must pay taxes.

a) A request
b) A law
c) A suggestion
d) An instruction

5. The train tracks meet at the **junction** just outside the city.

a) A station
b) A crossing
c) A destination
d) A terminal

6. The country **exports** large quantities of coffee to Europe.

a) Consumes
b) Produces
c) Sells abroad
d) Imports

7. The bridge is strong enough to **support** heavy vehicles.

a) Hold up
b) Create
c) Move
d) Design

8. She presented her **portfolio** to the art school for admission.

a) A collection of works
b) A book
c) A letter
d) A case

9. The author submitted her **manuscript** to the publisher.

a) A typed document
b) A handwritten document
c) An edited document
d) A printed document

10. The detective found **evidence** that linked the suspect to the crime.

a) Proof
b) Clue
c) Doubt
d) Report

Activity 3: Study the images provided, which illustrate various Greek roots along with example words underneath each image. Pay close attention to the Greek root and how it forms the basis for the meaning of each example word. This exercise will help you understand the connection between Greek roots and their English derivatives.

Astr

Star

Astronaut
Astronomy
Asteroid

Bio

Life

Biology
Biography
Antibiotic

Chron

Time

Chronological
Synchronize
Chronicle

Geo

Earth

Geography
Geometry
Geology

Graph

Write

Autograph
Graphics
Graphite

Hydr

Water

Hydration
Dehydrate
Hydroelectric

Log

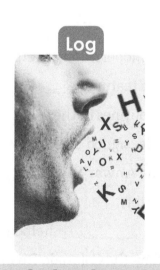

Word, Thought, Speech

Logic
Apology
Dialogue

Micr

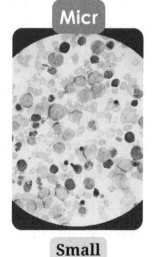

Small

Microscope
Microwave
Microchip

Activity 4: The word bank below contains Greek-derived words. Choose the most suitable word to complete each sentence by inferring its meaning from the context.

			Hydration
Antibiotics	Astronaut	Dialogue	Hydroelectric
Apology	Autobiography	Geology	Microchip
Asteroid	Chronicle	Graphics	Synchronized

1. "The Anglo-Saxon _____" is a historical record of events in Anglo-Saxon England, originally compiled on the orders of King Alfred the Great in the 9th century.

2. The discovery of penicillin by Alexander Fleming in 1928 marked the beginning of modern _____, revolutionizing the treatment of bacterial infections.

3. "The Diary of a Young Girl" by Anne Frank is a powerful _____ that chronicles her life and experiences during the Holocaust.

4. The Hoover Dam, completed in 1936, is one of the largest _____ power plants in the United States, providing electricity to millions of people.

5. In 2013, an _____ named 2012 DA14 passed within 17,200 miles of Earth, closer than many of our satellites.

6. In 1971, Intel introduced the first _____, the Intel 4004, which paved the way for the development of modern computers.

7. The 2020 Tokyo Olympics featured _____ swimming events where athletes performed perfectly timed routines in the water.

8. The Camp David Accords, signed in 1978, were a result of intense _____ between Egyptian President Anwar Sadat and Israeli Prime Minister Menachem Begin, facilitated by U.S. President Jimmy Carter.

9. The study of _____ helped scientists understand the formation of the Grand Canyon, which was carved by the Colorado River over millions of years.

10. The 1995 release of the movie "Toy Story" by Pixar was a milestone in the use of computer _____, being the first fully computer-animated feature film.

11. During the 2014 FIFA World Cup, players were allowed official water breaks to ensure proper _____ due to the high temperatures in Brazil.

12. In 1969, _____ Neil Armstrong became the first human to set foot on the moon during NASA's Apollo 11 mission, famously stating, "That's one small step for man, one giant leap for mankind."

13. In 2009, British Prime Minister Gordon Brown issued a formal _____ to Alan Turing, the pioneering computer scientist, for the government's treatment of him after World War II.

Activity 5: How many words can you find or remember from this lesson that have the Greek or Latin root in each circle?

Audi _____
_____
_____

Bio _____
_____
_____

Dict _____
_____
_____

Chron _____
_____
_____

Port _____
_____
_____

Graph _____
_____
_____

Script _____
_____
_____

Log _____
_____
_____

Vis _____
_____
_____

Geo _____
_____
_____

LESSON 41: Compound Roots

Did you know that words combining two or more Greek and Latin root words are called compound roots? These compound roots often mix prefixes, bases, and suffixes from Latin or Greek to create new words with specific meanings. We've already encountered a few in previous lessons, like "manuscript" (manu-hand /script-write), "export" (ex-out/port-carry), and "antibiotic" (anti-against/bio-life).

Now, it's time to dive deeper into the world of compound roots! We'll explore some of the most important roots that combine with other root words to create completely new meanings. By learning these roots, you'll be able to decode the meanings of complex words just by recognizing their Greek or Latin origins.

Some of the most important roots that combine with various words are: "**con**" (together), "**contra**" (against), "**pre**" (before), "**pro**" (forward), "**in**" (into, not), "**de**" (away from) and "**re**" (again). In this lesson we'll be exploring each of these and how they combine with other Greek and Latin root words.

Root Words		Modern Definition
con *Latin: with, together*	**struct** *Latin: to make up, build*	Construct: To build or form (something) by putting together parts or materials.
con *Latin: with, together*	**scrib/script** *Latin: write*	Conscript: To enroll by force, typically into military service.
con *Latin: with, together*	**ven** *Latin: come*	Convene: To come together for a meeting or activity.
contra *Latin: against*	**dict** *Latin: speak*	Contradict: To assert the opposite of a statement made by someone.

Root Words		Modern Definition
contra *Latin: against* + **ven** *Latin: come*		Contravene: To come against (a rule, law, or agreement), implying violation or conflict with something established.
pre *Latin: before* + **dict** *Latin: speak*		Predict: To say what will happen in the future (before it happens).
pre *Latin: before, for, forward* + **ven** *Latin: come*		Prevent: To stop something from happening (before it happens).
pro *Latin: before, for, forward* + **duc/duct** *Latin: lead, bring*		Produce: To create or bring forth. *(also "product")*
pro *Latin: before, for, forward* + **vid/vis** *Latin: see*		Provide: To supply or make available (to look ahead in order to make preparations). *(also "provision")*
in* *Latin: in, on* + **duc/duct** *Latin: lead, bring*		Induce: To cause or bring about. *(also "induction")*
in *Latin: in, on* + **scrib/script** *Latin: write*		Inscribe: To write or carve on a surface. *(also "inscription")*
in *Latin: in, on* + **spec/spect** *Latin: look closely*		Inspect: To look at closely to assess condition.
de *Latin: down, away, remove, reverse, about* + **duc/duct** *Latin: lead, bring*		Deduce: To reach a conclusion by reasoning. *(also "deduction")*

* Note that "in-" also signifies negation, as already discussed in Part 5 Prefixes and Suffixes.

Root Words		Modern Definition
de *Latin: down, away, remove, reverse, about*	**struct** *Latin: to make up, build*	Destruct: To destroy or demolish.
re *Latin: again, back*	**duc/duct** *Latin: lead, bring*	Reduce: To make smaller or less in amount. *(also "reduction")*
re *Latin: again, back*	**vid/vis** *Latin: see*	Revisit: To visit or examine again.

 Activity 1: Read the following historical account about the construction of the Colosseum in ancient Rome, and answer the questions that follow.

The Construction of the Colosseum

In ancient Rome, Emperor Vespasian initiated the construction of a grand arena. It would symbolize the empire's might and serve as a venue for public entertainment. This grand project would eventually become known as the Colosseum.

To produce the labor force required for such a massive undertaking, Vespasian's government conscripted thousands of slaves, many of whom are believed to have been prisoners of war. These conscripts were forced to convene at the construction site, where they toiled day and night to bring the emperor's vision to life.

Some senators opposed Vespasian's decisions, arguing that the funds for the Colosseum could be better used elsewhere. Despite their objections, the emperor pressed on, determined to defy the opposition and proceed with his grand design.

Predicting the immense popularity of the Colosseum, Vespasian's architects worked painstakingly to prevent any structural failures. They inspected every aspect of the construction, ensuring that the massive stone blocks were securely placed.

 Architects and engineers combined their respective expertise to determine the best methods for creating an arena that could withstand the test of time.

Throughout the construction process, various inscriptions were made on the stones, marking significant contributions and commemorating events. These inscriptions would later be revisited by historians and archaeologists to glean insights into the Colosseum's history.

Despite numerous obstacles, the Colosseum gradually took form. The project faced significant setbacks, as materials had to be transported from far-off locations, greatly increasing costs. Additionally, many workers faced the risk of permanent injury or even death.

Emperor Vespasian's successor, Titus, was present at the Colosseum's grand opening, where he witnessed the spectacular games and events that took place within its walls. These games were designed to induce awe and wonder in the spectators, showcasing Rome's power and ingenuity. The Colosseum, now complete, stood as the epitome of Roman engineering and the empire's ability to provide for its citizens' entertainment.

1. What is the primary goal of the construction mentioned in the passage?

a) To destroy ancient ruins

b) To provide a space for military training

c) To build a monumental arena for public entertainment

d) To create a new residential area

2. Who were the conscripts in the context of the Colosseum's construction?

a) Enslaved people and prisoners of war forced to work

b) Skilled architects from Greece

c) Wealthy citizens funding the project

d) Volunteer soldiers from the Roman army

3. What does "convene" imply about the workers at the construction site?

a) They were arguing constantly

b) They were leaving the site

c) They were scattering in different directions

d) They were assembling together to work

4. What is the significance of the inscriptions made on the stones?

a) They were used to mark the weight of the stones

b) They served as blueprints for construction

c) They recorded important milestones and donations made

d) They warned trespassers

5. How did architects and engineers ensure the Colosseum's durability?

a) By conducting religious ceremonies

b) By reducing the size of the arena

c) By halting construction during bad weather

d) By using their combined expertise to find the best construction methods

6. What is the meaning of "predicting" in this context?

a) Constructing a model

b) Foreseeing future success

c) Preventing structural failures

d) Inspecting the construction site

7. Which of the following best describes a challenge faced in the construction of the Colosseum?

a) Insufficient funding for the project

b) Delays due to political disagreements

c) Expensive transportation of material

d) Reduced workforce due to injury

8. What does "induce" mean regarding the games in the Colosseum?

a) To evoke a sense of amazement in the spectators

b) To destroy the arena

c) To prevent further construction

d) To defy the emperor's orders

9. Emperor Vespasian didn't survive to witness the grand opening. Why was this the case?

a) Because the Colosseum was completed much later.

b) Because the construction was halted for many years.

c) Because Emperor Vespasian lost interest in the project.

d) Because Titus was present as Vespasian's successor.

10. "The Colosseum, now complete, stood as the epitome of Roman engineering and the empire's ability to provide for its citizens' entertainment." What does this statement primarily highlight?

a) The architectural beauty of the Colosseum

b) The social and cultural importance of entertainment in Roman society

c) The technical and structural ingenuity of Roman engineers

d) The economic investment in public infrastructure by the Roman Empire

Part 7
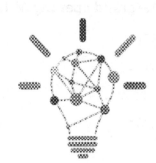
Synonyms and Antonyms

LESSON 42: Synonyms and Antonyms

 Ever wondered how words can be best friends or total opposites? Meet synonyms and antonyms! Synonyms are like word twins, sharing the same meaning, while antonyms are like word rivals, having completely opposite meanings.

Imagine "bright" and "shiny" giving each other a thumbs-up for being so alike, while "bright" and "dark" stand on opposite sides, showing how different they can be.

Why is it important to study synonyms and antonyms?

Studying synonyms and antonyms is important because it enhances our language skills in several ways. It improves vocabulary by providing a variety of words with similar or opposite meanings, which helps in making communication more precise and effective. This also enhances writing by preventing repetition and making it more engaging and interesting, while antonyms add contrast and depth for nuanced expression.

Recognizing synonyms and antonyms aids in understanding the context and meaning of unfamiliar words, thereby improving reading comprehension. Additionally, having a rich vocabulary enables clearer and more accurate expression in both speaking and writing. Furthermore, studying synonyms and antonyms can improve test performance, as many standardized tests include questions on these topics. In short, studying them enriches language abilities, making one a more effective communicator and better writer.

SYNONYMS: Words that have similar meanings
Examples:
Ancient - old, antique, aged, historic.
Amiable - friendly, pleasant, agreeable, affable.

ANTONYMS: Words that have opposite meanings
Examples:
Ancient: modern, new, recent, contemporary.
Amiable: unfriendly, unpleasant, disagreeable, hostile.

Activity 1: Choose the synonym that best matches the words we have encountered in previous lessons. Use the list of definitions to assist you.

Defiant	Mock
Quagmire	Comply
Deride	Sacred
Infuriate	Chaos
Abide	Rebellious
Inviolable	Enrage

Definitions

Defiant: Refusing to obey something or someone.

Quagmire: A difficult, complicated, or unpleasant situation that is hard to escape from.

Deride: To laugh at someone or something in a way that shows you think they are stupid or of no value.

Infuriate: To make someone extremely angry.

Abide: To accept and follow a rule, decision, or instruction.

Inviolable: Something that is so sacred or important that it must not be violated or disrespected.

 Activity 2: Identify the synonyms in each pair of sentences.

PAIR 1
A. The teenager was defiant, refusing to follow the school's strict dress code.
B. The teenager was rebellious, refusing to adhere to the school's strict dress code.

A._____   B._____

A._____   B._____

PAIR 2
A. The harsh critic's comments were meant to deride the artist's work, which only served to infuriate her loyal fans.
B. The bully's cruel actions to mock the student's appearance did nothing but enrage his friends.

A._____   B._____

A._____   B._____

Activity 3: Match each word with its correct synonym after reviewing the definitions provided.

- **Obscure**: Unclear or not well known or difficult to understand.

- **Obsolete**: Outdated or no longer in use.

- **Occurrence**: Something that happens or takes place.

- **Ominous**: Giving the impression that something bad is going to happen.

- **Oscillate**: To move or swing back and forth in a regular rhythm.

- **Overdue**: Not done, returned, or happening by the expected or required time.

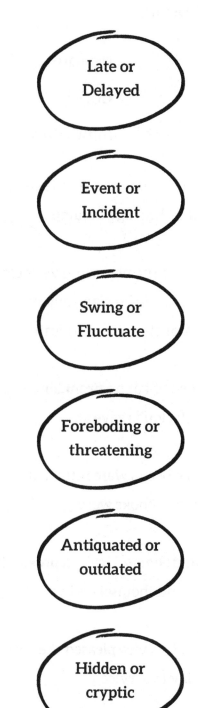

Late or Delayed

Event or Incident

Swing or Fluctuate

Foreboding or threatening

Antiquated or outdated

Hidden or cryptic

Activity 4: Complete each sentence by transforming it into its opposite meaning. Substitute the bolded word with its antonym, chosen from the word bank.

defiant	obscure	overdue
deride	obsolete	quagmire
infuriated	ominous	rebellious

\+ The old technology remained **relevant**, despite the advent of new innovations.

\- 1. The old technology became _____ with the advent of new innovations.

\+ The details of the plan were **very clear** to the committee members.

\- 2. The details of the plan remained _____ to the committee members due to the lack of clear communication.

\+ The clear skies gave a **promising** feeling as the sun shone brightly.

\- 3. The dark clouds gave an _____ feeling before the storm.

\+ The library books were returned **on time**.

\- 4. The library books were _____ and needed to be returned immediately.

\+ They found themselves in a **prosperity** of wealth after the business succeeded.

\- 5. They found themselves in a _____ of debt after the business failed.

\+ The prompt service **pleased** the customers.

\- 6. The delay in service _____ the customers.

\+ The critic did not hesitate to **praise** the artist's latest work.

\- 7. The critic did not hesitate to _____ the artist's latest work.

\+ The **obedient** teenager was **compliant** with the school rules.

\- 8. The _____ teenager was _____ of the school rules.

LESSON 43: Contextual Synonyms

Did you know that not all synonyms can be swapped in every situation? Even though synonyms have similar meanings, choosing the right one is crucial because it can change the tone or clarity of a sentence.

For example, the words "happy" and "ecstatic" both describe positive emotions, but "ecstatic" is much stronger and more intense than "happy." Consider these two sentences:

She was happy to see her friends after a long break.
She was ecstatic when she won the grand prize in the lottery.

In the first sentence, the word "happy" indicates a pleasant, positive emotion. It shows that the person is glad and content to be reunited with her friends, but the emotion is relatively mild and common.

In the second sentence, the word "ecstatic" conveys a much stronger and more intense feeling. It suggests overwhelming joy and excitement, much more than just being happy. Winning a grand prize in the lottery is a significant event that evokes an intense emotional reaction, which is why "ecstatic" is the more appropriate word to use in this context.

Using the right synonym ensures that your message is clear and conveys the exact emotion or meaning you intend. In this lesson, we'll explore how context influences the choice of synonyms and why it's important to pick the most suitable one for each situation.

In previous lessons, we encountered a variety of Tier 2 vocabulary words. In this lesson, we will explore a selection of these words along with their synonyms and learn how to use them effectively in context. By understanding the nuances of their synonyms, you will enhance your writing and communication skills. In our next lesson, we will explore the antonyms of these words.

Here is the list of words we will be focusing on, along with their synonyms:

Severe	Harsh, Intense
Independent	Self-reliant, Autonomous
Endurance	Stamina, Perseverance
Maneuver	Navigate, Move
Appreciate	Value, Recognize
Antagonize	Provoke, Irritate
Catalyst	Stimulus, Trigger
Fallacy	Misconception, Error
Malady	Illness, Disease
Catastrophe	Disaster, Calamity

 **Activity 1:** Read the following explanation about the nuances of words, followed by the examples. This will help you understand how to choose specific synonyms to convey the exact message you want.

Understanding the Nuances of Words.

"Nuances" refers to the subtle differences or shades of meaning between similar words. Understanding nuances helps in choosing the most precise word to convey the exact emotion, tone, or context intended in a sentence.

For example, the words "disaster" and "calamity" are synonyms of "catastrophe." However, each word has a slightly different nuance. Let's consider the following sentence:

> *The hurricane caused a **catastrophe** in the coastal city, leaving thousands homeless.*

The word "catastrophe" in this sentence emphasizes the large-scale devastation and severe impact of the event.

Now consider the following sentence using the synonym "disaster" instead:

> *The hurricane caused a **disaster** in the coastal city, leaving thousands homeless.*

"Disaster" is a more general term that indicates a sudden, damaging event. It doesn't inherently convey the same level of magnitude as "catastrophe," but it still implies significant harm and disruption.

Finally, consider the synonym "calamity" used in the same sentence:

> *The hurricane caused a **calamity** in the coastal city, leaving thousands homeless.*

"Calamity" emphasizes the resulting distress and suffering. It often suggests a personal or emotional impact, focusing more on the human toll than on the physical destruction alone.

By understanding these nuances, you can choose the most appropriate word to precisely convey your intended meaning.

Activity 2: Choose the most appropriate word from the list to complete each sentence. Pay attention to the context, and write your chosen word in the blank space. Then check your answers and explanation on page 273.

1. Despite the _____ of the desert heat, the explorers continued their journey. **Target Word: Severity | Synonyms: Harshness, Intensity.**

2. The student's _____ during the marathon was impressive, showing both physical and mental strength. **Target Word: Endurance | Synonyms: Stamina, Perseverance.**

3. The scientist served as a _____ for the project, inspiring his team to think creatively. **Target Word: Catalyst | Synonyms: Stimulus, Trigger.**

4. His decision to drop out of school was based on a common _____, that you don't need education to succeed. **Target Word: Fallacy | Synonyms: Misconception, Error.**

5. The small non-profit organization operated _____, relying on donations and volunteer work. **Target Word: Independently | Synonyms: Self-reliantly, Autonomously.**

6. To _____ through the dense forest, they had to follow the marked trails carefully. **Target Word: Maneuver | Synonyms: Navigate, Move.**

7. The manager tried not to _____ the employees, understanding that a happy workforce is more productive. **Target Word: Antagonize | Synonyms: Provoke, Irritate.**

8. She didn't fully _____ the significance of the gesture until much later. **Target Word: Appreciate | Synonyms: Value, Recognize.**

9. The outbreak of the _____ spread quickly, affecting a large part of the population. **Target Word: Malady | Synonyms: Illness, Disease.**

LESSON 44: Contextual Antonyms

In a previous lesson we encountered the sentence "They found themselves in a **prosperity** of wealth after the business succeeded." Here you had to find the most suitable antonym that would make sense to change the sentence into its opposite: They found themselves in a **quagmire** of debt after the business failed. However, if you consider the words "prosperity" and "quagmire" outside any context, you wouldn't say that they are antonyms. But when putting them in context, as in these two sentences, they make perfect sense and "quagmire" serves to convey the meaning that they were not wealthy at all.

The Importance of Context in Identifying Antonyms

Context plays a crucial role in determining the appropriate antonym. Words can have multiple meanings and connotations, and their opposites may vary depending on the situation in which they are used. When we look at words within a specific context, we can more accurately identify their antonyms and understand the nuances of their meanings. This lesson will focus on how to determine the most suitable antonyms based on the context of a sentence or passage.

1. Understanding Context:

The meaning of a word can change depending on the context. It is important to read the entire sentence or passage to grasp the full meaning.

Example: "Severe" in the context of weather might have different antonyms compared to "severe" in the context of a punishment.

Weather:
The **severe** weather caused significant damage.
Antonym: The **mild** weather caused minimal damage.

Punishment:
The teacher's **severe** criticism upset the student.
Antonym: The teacher's **gentle** criticism encouraged the student.

2. Choosing the Right Antonym:

Not all antonyms are interchangeable. The right antonym must fit the context to convey the intended opposite meaning.

Example: For "bright," the appropriate antonym can vary based on the context.

Intelligence (as synonym for "bright"):

She is a **bright** student who excels in all her subjects.
Antonym: She is a **dull** student who struggles in all her subjects.

In the context of intelligence, "dull" contrasts with "bright" to indicate a lack of sharpness or quickness in understanding.

Describing Color:

The painting is full of **bright** colors that catch the eye.
Antonym: The painting is full of **dull** colors that blend into the background.

In terms of color, "dull" is the appropriate antonym to describe colors that are not vivid or vibrant.

Describing Light:

The room was **bright** with sunlight streaming through the windows.
Antonym: The room was **dim** with only a small lamp for light.

For light, "dim" is a more precise antonym for "bright," as it describes a low level of light.

We typically do not say "a dull room" to describe a room with low light. Instead, we use "dim" or "dark" to describe the lighting. "Dull" is more commonly used to describe lack of vividness or excitement in colors or activities.

3. Nuances and Degrees of Meaning

Some words have nuanced meanings that require specific antonyms to accurately convey the opposite idea.

Example: "Endurance" implies lasting through hardship, so "weakness" or "fatigue" are suitable antonyms, each adding a slightly different nuance.

Endurance:
His **endurance** during the marathon was impressive.
Opposite: His **weakness** during the marathon was evident.

She showed great **endurance** despite the long hours.
Opposite: She showed great **fatigue** despite the short hours.

"Weakness" is appropriate in the first example because it directly contrasts with the physical and mental strength implied by "endurance." In the context of a marathon, "weakness" suggests an inability to sustain effort, highlighting a lack of strength or resilience.

In the second example, "fatigue" is more suitable because it emphasizes tiredness and exhaustion rather than a general lack of strength. Using "weakness" would suggest an overall lack of strength, which is not the intended meaning. "Fatigue" specifically refers to the tiredness experienced after working short hours. The phrase "despite the short hours" highlights that she became very tired even with less time, contrasting directly with enduring long hours without tiring.

In the last two lessons, we have discussed synonyms and antonyms, emphasizing the importance of their nuanced meanings and usage. We have seen how context determines the most suitable synonym or antonym to convey the intended meaning accurately.

We will now practice an activity on antonyms, followed by an activity on synonyms and antonyms, using Tier 2 words already encountered in previous lessons, to reinforce your learning and usage. The answers to these activities will be accompanied by explanations. This will help you not only understand the words better but also use them more effectively in your writing and communication.

Activity 1: The following sentences contain words in bold that do not fit the context of the sentence. Choose the appropriate antonym from the list below, which conveys the intended message in each sentence. Then check the answers and explanation on page 274.

ANTONYMS		ANTONYMS	
Antagonize:	Soothe, Pacify	Fallacy:	Truth, Fact
Appreciation:	Disregard, Dismiss	Independent:	Dependent, Reliant
Catalyst:	Hindrance, Obstacle	Malady:	Health, Wellness
Catastrophe:	Success, Blessing	Maneuver:	Stumble, Hesitate
Endurance:	Weakness, Fatigue	Severe:	Mild, Gentle

1. They **appreciated** his suggestion without even considering its potential benefits.

Correct: They _____ his suggestion without even considering its potential benefits.

2. The child was so **independent** on his parents that he couldn't make decisions on his own.

Correct: The child was so _____ on his parents that he couldn't make decisions on his own.

3. After only a few hours of hiking, she felt extreme **weakness** and needed to rest.

Correct: After only a few hours of hiking, she felt extreme _____ and needed to rest.

4. The lack of funding was a major **catalyst** to the project's progress.

Correct: The lack of funding was a major _____ to the project's progress.

5. The **mild** weather caused the city to shut down all services.

Correct: The _____ weather caused the city to shut down all services.

6. The **fallacy** about the incident finally came to light, clearing up many misunderstandings.

Correct: The _____ about the incident finally came to light, clearing up many misunderstandings.

Antagonize:	Soothe, Pacify	Fallacy:	Truth, Fact
Appreciation:	Disregard, Dismiss	Independent:	Dependent, Reliant
Catalyst:	Hindrance, Obstacle	Malady:	Health, Wellness
Catastrophe:	Success, Blessing	Maneuver:	Stumble, Hesitate
Endurance:	Weakness, Fatigue	Severe:	Mild, Gentle

7. Her sense of **malady** improved significantly after she started meditating daily.

Correct: Her sense of _____ improved significantly after she started meditating daily.

8. Winning the scholarship was a **catastrophe**, allowing her to attend college without financial worries.

Correct: Winning the scholarship was a _____, allowing her to attend college without financial worries.

9. She was **independent** on her tutor for help with every assignment.

Correct: She was _____ on her tutor for help with every assignment.

10. He **maneuvered** over his words during the presentation, losing the audience's attention.

Correct: He _____ over his words during the presentation, losing the audience's attention.

11. She **maneuvered** before answering the question, unsure of her response.

Correct: She _____ before answering the question, unsure of her response.

12. The committee **appreciated** her concerns as irrelevant to the discussion.

Correct: The committee _____ her concerns as irrelevant to the discussion.

13. The gentle music helped to **antagonize** the anxious crowd.

Correct: The gentle music helped to _____ the anxious crowd.

Antagonize: Soothe, Pacify

Appreciation: Disregard, Dismiss

Catalyst: Hindrance, Obstacle

Catastrophe: Success, Blessing

Endurance: Weakness, Fatigue

Fallacy: Truth, Fact

Independent: Dependent, Reliant

Malady: Health, Wellness

Maneuver: Stumble, Hesitate

Severe: Mild, Gentle

14. The cat's **severe** purring was very soothing to the children.

Correct: The cat's _____ purring was very soothing to the children.

15. The new marketing strategy was a huge **catastrophe**, increasing sales dramatically.

Correct: The new marketing strategy was a huge _____, increasing sales dramatically.

16. Regular exercise and a balanced diet contribute greatly to good **malady**.

Correct: Regular exercise and a balanced diet contribute greatly to good _____.

17. The **fallacy** that the Earth orbits the Sun is well-established in science.

Correct: The _____ that the Earth orbits the Sun is well-established in science.

18. The strict regulations acted as a **catalyst** to the company's expansion plans.

Correct: The strict regulations acted as an _____ to the company's expansion plans.

19. The diplomat's calming words were able to **antagonize** the angry protesters.

Correct: The diplomat's calming words were able to _____ the angry protesters.

20. His **fatigue** became apparent when he couldn't lift the weights he used to handle with ease.

Correct: His _____ became apparent when he couldn't lift the weights he used to handle with ease.

LESSON 45: Expanding Your Synonym and Antonym Vocabulary

Understanding and using a rich vocabulary of synonyms and antonyms is crucial for effective communication and writing. In previous lessons, we have practiced various Tier 2 vocabulary words along with their synonyms and antonyms. It's important to continue expanding your vocabulary to express and understand ideas and concepts more clearly, which will improve your reading comprehension and sharpen your writing skills.

In this lesson, you will be provided with a list of additional Tier 2 vocabulary words along with their synonyms and antonyms. By studying and learning these additional words, you will further develop your language skills and be better prepared to tackle complex texts and articulate your thoughts more clearly.

How to Learn and Study Additional Synonyms and Antonyms

1. Review the List: Carefully read through the provided list of Tier 2 vocabulary words, along with their synonyms and antonyms.

2. Identify Unknown Words: Note any unfamiliar words and look up their definitions.

3. Write Definitions: Write down the definitions of each word, including their synonyms and antonyms.

4. Create Example Sentences: Write sentences using each word and its synonyms and antonyms to understand their usage in different contexts.

5. Daily Vocabulary Practice: Spend a few minutes each day reviewing and practicing the new words.

6. Practice Writing: Incorporate the new vocabulary words in your writing assignments and practice essays.

7. Contextual Understanding: Notice how these words are used in the books, articles, and other texts you read.

Keep a Vocabulary Journal: Maintain a journal or notebook where you record the words, their definitions, example sentences, and any notes on their usage. Review this journal regularly to reinforce your learning.

8. Use Flashcards: Make flashcards with the word on one side and its definition, synonyms, and antonyms on the other. Review regularly.

9. Seek Feedback: Share your sentences and writings with a teacher or parent/ and ask for feedback.

Tier 2 Vocabulary	Synonyms	Antonyms
Ancient	Old, Antique	Modern, New
Amiable	Friendly, Pleasant	Unfriendly, Hostile
Apprehend	Arrest, Capture	Release, Free
Debate	Discuss, Argue	Agree, Concur
Extreme	Intense, Severe	Moderate, Mild
Invoke	Call upon, Summon	Revoke, Withdraw
Defiant	Rebellious, Uncooperative	Compliant, Obedient
Obsolete	Outdated, Antiquated	Modern, Current, Valid
Infuriate	Enrage, Anger	Calm, Soothe
Obscure	Unclear, Vague	Clear, Obvious
Provoke	Incite, Agitate	Calm, Soothe
Ominous	Threatening, Foreboding	Promising, Encouraging, Auspicious
Grotesque	Distorted, Ugly	Beautiful, Attractive
Fundamental	Basic, Essential	Secondary, Unimportant
Efficient	Effective, Competent	Inefficient, Wasteful
Robust	Strong, Sturdy	Weak, Fragile

Part 8

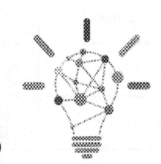

Homophones and Frequently Misspelled Words

LESSON 46: Introduction to Homophones

Homophones are words that sound the same but have different meanings and often different spellings. For example, "to," "two," and "too" are homophones. They can be tricky because even though they sound identical, their meanings and spellings are different, which can lead to confusion when writing and reading.

Why are homophones important?

Understanding homophones is crucial for several reasons:
1. **Clarity in Writing**: Using the correct homophone ensures that your writing is clear and conveys the intended meaning.
2. **Improving Spelling Skills**: Learning homophones helps improve your spelling skills, as you need to distinguish between words that sound the same.
3. **Enhanced Reading Comprehension**: Knowing homophones can improve your ability to understand context and meaning in reading, as you can identify which word fits the context of a sentence.
4. **Effective Communication**: Proper use of homophones helps in avoiding misunderstandings in written communication.

This lesson will focus on two categories of homophones. The first category includes fundamental words like "your" and "you're," and "there" and "they're," which you should already be familiar with. The second category will introduce more complex, Tier 2 vocabulary homophones that are frequently misused or misspelled. By thoroughly understanding and practicing these homophones, you will build a solid foundation that enhances your reading comprehension and writing precision.

In the next part of the book, we will be focusing on writing and reading. Fully grasping these homophones will be crucial as we move forward, ensuring that you have the skills needed to express your ideas clearly and accurately.

Bare/Bear

Flower/Flour

Male/Mail

Activity 1: Review the table containing basic homophones and their example sentences. Note any words you feel need further study and practice. Write these words down in the first column of the next table.

Bear	Bare
While hiking, they saw a **bear** in the forest.	He asked her to **bare** her soul during their heart-to-heart conversation.
Break	**Brake**
She needed a **break** after studying for four hours straight.	He hit the **brake** when a deer jumped onto the road.
Dye	**Die**
She decided to **dye** her hair purple for the summer concert.	The old tree will **die** if it doesn't get enough water.
Fair	**Fare**
He argued that it wasn't **fair** for everyone to get the same reward regardless of effort.	The taxi **fare** from the airport to the hotel was surprisingly affordable.

Heal	Heel	He'll
It will take time for her sprained ankle to **heal**.	The puppy finally learned to **heel** during walks.	**He'll** visit the museum next weekend. ("he **will**")

Heard	Herd
She **heard** a strange noise coming from the basement.	The shepherd moved the **herd** of sheep across the field.

Whole	Hole
She ate the **whole** pizza by herself.	He dug a **hole** in the backyard to plant the tree.
Lead	Led
The pipes in the old house are made of **lead**.	She **led** her team to a victory in the finals.
Pair	Pear
I need a new **pair** of shoes for the trip.	He enjoyed a juicy **pear** during lunch.
Passed	Past
He **passed** the difficult math test with flying colors.	In the **past**, people used horses for transportation.
Peace	Piece
The treaty brought **peace** to the warring nations.	Could I have another **piece** of that delicious cake?
Peak	Peek
The climbers reached the **peak** of the mountain just before noon.	Take a **peek** at the gifts before the party starts!
Waste	Waist
Don't **waste** your time worrying about things you can't control.	She measured her **waist** before ordering the custom dress.

There	Their	They're
There are many reasons why I love summer	**Their** new puppy is absolutely adorable.	**They're** planning to visit Europe next year. ("they **are**")

Seem		Seam
It might **seem** difficult at first, but you'll get used to it.		The **seam** of her dress came undone just before the concert.

Serial		Cereal
The police caught the **serial** offender last night.		For breakfast, he usually has a bowl of **cereal**.

Sight	Site	Cite
The Grand Canyon is a breathtaking **sight**.	The construction **site** was busy with workers.	Remember to **cite** your sources in your research paper.

Whether		Weather
Whether or not you agree, the project will proceed.		The **weather** forecast predicts rain for tomorrow.

Right		Write
You were **right** about the shortcut to the library.		Please **write** your name at the top of the worksheet.

Loose		Lose
The screw in the chair is **loose** and needs tightening.		Don't **lose** hope, even if things seem difficult right now.

Here	Hear
Please place your books **here** on this table.	Can you **hear** the thunder in the distance?

Your	You're
Is this **your** book on the table?	**You're** going to be amazed by the ending of the movie. ("you **are**")

Scent	Sent	Cent
The **scent** of fresh pine filled the air.	She **sent** the email last night.	He picked up a 5-**cent** coin from the sidewalk.

 **Activity 2:** Now that you've identified and listed the words in the first column of the table, look up their definitions if needed. Then, compose a sentence for each word that you have chosen.

Chosen Word	Definition	Sentence

195

Chosen Word	Definition	Sentence

LESSON 47: Advanced Homophones

The homophones chosen for this lesson are considered advanced due to their nuanced differences in meaning and usage. These words frequently appear in academic, professional, and formal writing, making them essential for clear and precise communication. For instance, words like "affect" and "effect" or "complement" and "compliment" are often misused because they sound similar but carry distinct meanings and implications. Mistaking these can lead to misunderstandings and inaccuracies in both personal and academic contexts.

Moreover, some pairs of homophones we will be studying, such as "capital" and "capitol," involve terms specific to certain fields or contexts where correct usage is crucial to convey accurate information about economics and government.

By studying these advanced homophones, you will develop a deeper understanding of English vocabulary and improve your ability to communicate effectively. This knowledge will aid in your academic writing, enhance your performance on standardized tests, and boost your overall confidence in using the English language.

This lesson will guide you through these pairs of homophones with definitions, examples, and exercises designed to test and reinforce your understanding.

Activity 1: Review the following homophones and their definitions. Try associating each homophone with the visual image provided to help retain these words.

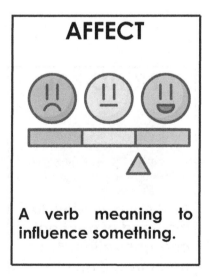

AFFECT

A verb meaning to influence something.

EFFECT

A noun meaning the result or outcome of an influence.

197

CAPITAL

Refers to wealth or resources, or a city that serves as a seat of government.

CAPITOL

Specifically refers to a building where a legislative body meets.

COMPLEMENT

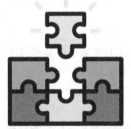

A noun or verb meaning something that completes or goes well with something.

COMPLIMENT

A noun or verb referring to a polite expression of praise or admiration.

PRINCIPLE

A noun meaning a fundamental truth or proposition that serves as the foundation for a system of belief.

PRINCIPAL

As a noun, it refers to the head of a school or organization. As an adjective, it means main or most important.

COARSE

An adjective describing a rough or loose texture or grain.

COURSE

Can refer to the path or direction something follows, or a series of lectures or lessons.

ACCEPT

A verb meaning to receive or agree to something.

EXCEPT

A preposition used to exclude something or someone.

STATIONARY

An adjective meaning not moving.

STATIONERY

A noun referring to writing materials, like paper and pens.

Activity 2: Complete the following sentences by choosing the correct homophone from each pair of sentences.

Coarse / Course

1. She signed up for a short _____ in digital marketing.

2. The towels were made from a very _____ material.

Affect / Effect

3. The _____ of the new policy on employee morale was noticeable immediately.

4. The new manager's leadership style will _____ the team's performance.

Capital / Capitol

5. The startup is seeking additional _____ to fund its expansion.

6. The protest took place outside the state _____ building.

Accept / Except

7. He decided to _____ the job offer after much consideration.

8. All students, _____ John, must submit their essays by Friday.

Complement / Compliment

9. He received a _____ on his new haircut.

10. The chef used fresh herbs to _____ the flavors in the dish.

Principle / Principal

11. The scientist refused to compromise his _____ during the debate.

12. The _____ of the school is retiring at the end of the year.

Stationary / Stationery

13. She wrote her thank-you notes on personalized _____.

14. The artwork should remain _____ to avoid damage.

Activity 3: Review the second set of homophones and their definitions. Associating each homophone with the visual image provided will help you better retain these words.

DESERT

As a noun, it refers to a barren area of land; as a verb, it means to abandon.

DESSERT

A noun referring to the sweet course eaten at the end of a meal.

ELICIT

A verb meaning to draw out a response or fact from someone in reaction to one's own actions or questions.

ILLICIT

An adjective describing something illegal or not permitted.

ENSURE

A verb meaning to make certain that something will occur.

INSURE

A verb meaning to secure or protect something, especially with insurance.

FURTHER

An adverb or adjective meaning additional or more.

FARTHER

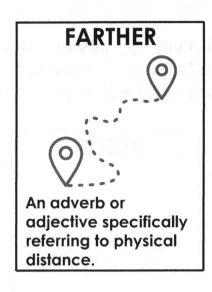

An adverb or adjective specifically referring to physical distance.

PRECEDE

A verb meaning to come before something in time or order.

PROCEED

A verb meaning to begin or continue with an action.

DEVICE

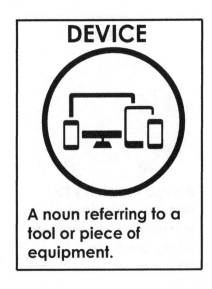

A noun referring to a tool or piece of equipment.

DEVISE

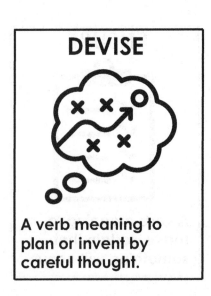

A verb meaning to plan or invent by careful thought.

Activity 4: Complete the following sentences by choosing the correct homophone from each pair of sentences.

Desert / Dessert

1. Many animals have adapted to survive in the harsh _____ conditions.

2. Chocolate cake is her favorite _____ after dinner.

Elicit / Illicit

3. The speaker's question was meant to _____ a reaction from the audience.

4. They were arrested for trading _____ substances.

Ensure / Insure

5. He decided to _____ his car against theft.

6. Please double-check the figures to _____ accuracy in the report.

Further / Farther

7. Is the parking lot much _____ from here?

8. This study aims to _____ our understanding of climate change.

Precede / Proceed

9. Please _____ to the next chapter after completing the exercises.

10. The opening remarks will _____ the award ceremony.

Device / Devise

11. You can track your daily steps with this small wearable _____.

12. We need to _____ a strategy to improve our sales numbers.

Activity 5: Choose the correct word to complete each sentence.

1. They need to _____ a new strategy to solve the problem.
a) devise
b) device

2. The medication did not _____ his condition as expected.
a) effect
b) affect

3. The introductory speech will _____ the main event.
a) proceed
b) precede

4. Her dress perfectly _____ the color of her eyes.
a) complemented
b) complimented

5. To _____ your understanding of the topic, you should read additional materials.
a) farther
b) further

6. He refused to compromise his _____, even when offered a large sum of money.
a) principle
b) principal

7. Everyone attended the meeting _____ for John.
a) except
b) accept

8. Please _____ that all windows are closed before you leave.
a) ensure
b) insure

9. The sandpaper was too _____ for the delicate surface.
a) course
b) coarse

10. The teacher's question was designed to _____ thoughtful responses from the students.
a) illicit
b) elicit

11. The police are cracking down on _____ activities in the area.
a) elicit
b) illicit

12. She ordered a chocolate _____ for dessert.
a) desert
b) dessert

13. The old machinery in the factory has remained _____ for years.
a) stationary
b) stationery

LESSON 48: Tricky Spelling Words

In this lesson we will explore a selection of words that are commonly misspelled due to their complex and tricky letters. We'll cover a variety of words from different categories, including scientific terms like "antibiotics," descriptive words like "grotesque," and action-oriented words like "maneuver." We'll also look at abstract concepts such as "conscience" and medical terms like "psychotherapy." These words have been chosen because they are frequently misspelled, and understanding their correct spelling will enhance your overall writing abilities.

For easier reference and study, these words are organized into distinct categories. This approach allows you to concentrate on one set of words at a time. Additionally, the challenging parts of the words are highlighted for easy identification. Each term will be accompanied by its definition and a brief explanation of what makes its spelling tricky.

After reviewing each word, complete the subsequent spelling practice to reinforce your learning. Keep track of any words you find particularly challenging and may need to practice further.

Activity 1: Review the words and their definitions in each category. Pay close attention to the underlined letters in each word. Then, write each word twice for spelling practice. Make sure to allocate at least 30 minutes for this activity.

Scientific and Technical Terms
Antibiotic • <u>Definition</u>: A medicine that inhibits the growth of or destroys microorganisms. • <u>Tricky elements</u>: the combination of "anti-" with "biotic"; the "io." SPELL _____ _____
Anticorrosive <u>Definition</u>: Preventing or inhibiting corrosion. <u>Tricky elements</u>: the combination of "anti-" with "corrosive"; the double "r" and the "s." SPELL _____ _____

Antioxidant

- Definition: A substance that inhibits oxidation, especially one used to counteract the deterioration of stored food products.
- Tricky elements: the combination of "anti-" with "oxidant"; "oxi" and "ant."

SPELL _____ _____

Asteroid

- Definition: A small rocky body orbiting the sun, commonly found between the orbits of Mars and Jupiter.
- Tricky elements: the combination of "aster-" with "-oid."

SPELL _____ _____

Astronaut
- Definition: A person who is trained to travel in a spacecraft.
- Tricky elements: the combination of "astro-" with "naut"; the "au."

SPELL _____ _____

Synchronize

- Definition: Cause to occur or operate at the same time or rate.
- Tricky elements: the letter combination "chr."

SPELL _____ _____

Medical Terms

Pneumonia

- Definition: An infection that inflames the air sacs in one or both lungs, which may fill with fluid.
- Tricky elements: the silent "p" at the beginning; the combination of the consonants "pn" and the vowels "eu."

SPELL _____ _____

Psychology

- <u>Definition</u>: The scientific study of the human mind and its functions, especially those affecting behavior in a given context.
- <u>Tricky elements</u>: the silent "p" at the beginning; the combination of "psy" and "ch."

SPELL _____ _____

Psychotherapy

- <u>Definition</u>: The treatment of mental disorder by psychological rather than medical means.
- <u>Tricky elements</u>: the silent "p" at the beginning; the combination of "psy" and the "ch"; the combination of "psycho-" with "therapy."

SPELL _____ _____

Abstract Terms

Apartheid

- <u>Definition</u>: A policy or system of segregation or discrimination on grounds of race.
- <u>Tricky elements</u>: the combination of "apart-" and "heid"; the "ei" in "heid."

SPELL _____ _____

Applicable

- Definition: Relevant or appropriate.
- Tricky elements: the double "p."

SPELL _____ _____

Conscience

- Definition: An inner feeling or voice viewed as acting as a guide to the rightness or wrongness of one's behavior.
- Tricky elements: the letter combination "scie."

SPELL _____ _____

Equilibrium

- Definition: A state in which opposing forces or influences are balanced.
- Tricky elements: the letter combination in "equi" and "rium."

SPELL _____ _____

Inviolable

- Definition: Never to be broken, infringed, or dishonored.
- Tricky elements: the letter combination in "vio."

SPELL _____ _____

Pseudonym

- Definition: A fictitious name, especially one used by an author.
- Tricky elements: the silent "p" at the beginning; the combination of "ps" and "eu"; the "y" in "nym."

SPELL _____ _____

Sovereign

- Definition: A supreme ruler, especially a monarch.
- Tricky elements: the pronunciation that does not clearly match the spelling because the "e" in "ver" is silent; the letter combination in "eign."

SPELL _____ _____

Subtlety

- Definition: The quality of being difficult to notice or understand; not obvious.
- Tricky elements: the silent "b"; the letter combination "btl" and "ety."

SPELL _____ _____

Descriptive Terms

Accessible

- Definition: Easy to approach, reach, enter, or use.
- Tricky elements: the double "c" and double "s."

SPELL _____ _____

Deceitful

- Definition: Guilty of or involving deceit; deceiving or misleading others.
- Tricky elements: the letter combination in "ceit."

SPELL _____ _____

Grotesque

- Definition: Comically or repulsively ugly or distorted.
- Tricky elements: the "esque" ending.

SPELL _____ _____

Poignant

- Definition: Evoking a keen sense of sadness or regret.
- Tricky elements: the silent "g"; the letter combination "oi" and "gn."

SPELL _____ _____

Surveillance

- Definition: Close observation, especially of a suspected spy or criminal.
- Tricky elements: the "u" in "sur"; the letter combination "vei" and the double "l."

SPELL _____ _____

Action-Oriented Terms

Contravene

- Definition: To go against or act in conflict with.
- Tricky elements: the combination of "contra-" and "vene"; the letter combination in "vene."

SPELL _____ _____

Enthrall

- Definition: To capture the fascinated attention of.
- Tricky elements: the combination of "th" and "rall"; the double "l" ending.

SPELL _____ _____

Maneuver

- Definition: A movement or series of moves requiring skill and care.
- Tricky elements: the letter combination "eu."

SPELL _____ _____

Vanquish

- Definition: To defeat thoroughly.
- Tricky elements: the "q" in "quish"; the ending "quish."

SPELL _____ _____

Part 9

Writing and Reading

LESSON 49: Writing Narrative Texts

What is a narrative text? In essence, a narrative text recounts a story in which the central character, known as the "protagonist," faces a challenge. It describes the actions taken by the protagonist, how they dealt with this challenge, and whether or not they were successful in overcoming it.

Typically, when you write a story, you aim for it to be read by others. You strive to make your story engaging and captivating. But how can we write a story that truly resonates? We must select words that enable the reader to "visualize" the story unfolding in their imagination and to empathize with the protagonist's experiences. This is achieved by employing descriptive language that vividly captures the setting, the events, the protagonist's feelings, and the emotions being expressed.

What are the main aims of narrative writing?

- **Tell a Story:** Narrative writing involves telling a story, which may be based on real-life events or be entirely fictional. It unfolds over time and concludes with a resolution, whether it's overcoming a challenge, finding a solution, or even experiencing a tragedy.

- **Develop Characters:** The characters in your story should feel real to the reader. Each character should have a distinct personality, complete with emotions, beliefs, and opinions. Throughout the story, these characters should undergo development or growth.

- **Create Atmosphere and Setting:** The setting is where and when your story takes place, providing the backdrop against which the drama unfolds. Effective narratives paint vivid worlds that envelop the reader, allowing them to immerse themselves in another life or environment.

- **Convey a Theme or Message:** Great narratives often carry underlying themes or messages that resonate with the reader. These themes provide deeper insights into life, society, or human nature.

- **Evoke Emotions:** A compelling story evokes the reader's emotions—joy, sadness, excitement, or fear—and establishes an emotional connection. This emotional engagement is crucial in keeping the reader invested in the story.

How do we begin writing a story? Writing a story involves two distinct phases: (i) the planning phase and (ii) the writing phase. During the planning phase, you determine the title, the setting, the main characters, and the narrator of the story. In the writing phase, you concentrate on gradually developing the narrative.

Below, you will see a table designed to assist you during the planning phase of your narrative. This table outlines the essential elements to consider while planning your story. We will discuss the writing phase and its corresponding table after we have completed the reading comprehension exercise and its analysis.

Story Planning Table

ELEMENT	DESCRIPTION	DETAILS TO CONSIDER
Title	Decide on a title that captures the essence of your story.	• What does the title reveal about the story? Does it intrigue the reader?
Setting	Determine where and when the story takes place.	• How does the setting influence the story? What mood or atmosphere does it create?
Main Characters	Identify the protagonist and other central characters.	• What are their personalities, motivations, and roles in the story? How will they evolve?
Point of View	Choose the narrator or point of view for the story.	• Will it be first-person or third-person? How does this choice impact the story's presentation?
Plot	Outline the major events and sequence.	• What are the key conflicts? • How will the story progress towards the climax and resolution?

Activity 1: On the next page, you'll read a story about Noah's quest for a lost pirate's treasure. This activity has two goals:

1. **Observe Narrative Elements:** Notice how narrative elements like character, setting, and plot are integrated within the story.
2. **Test Comprehension:** Answer questions to assess your understanding of the story.

How to Proceed:

• **While Reading:** Focus on how the story develops progressively.

• **After Reading:** Complete the provided questions about the story's details.

Reading Comprehension 1: Narrative Text

The Lost Treasure of Blackbeard

Noah had spent years searching for the fabled map of Blackbeard's Treasure. His relentless quest had finally led him to a remote, abandoned old pub in Yorkshire, England. It was here, amidst the dust and cobwebs, that he unearthed the ancient parchment. His heart raced with exhilaration as he unfolded the map, revealing that the legendary treasure was buried on the remote Scottish island of Fair Isle. The intricate details and aged ink filled him with awe, knowing he was on the brink of an extraordinary discovery.

Determined to claim the treasure, Noah hired a fishing boat and a seasoned skipper to take him to Fair Isle. The boat, chosen for its inconspicuous appearance and plain image, was old and not particularly safe. As they ventured into the vicious North Sea, the boat's age became painfully apparent. The journey was perilous; they battled towering waves and fierce winds, losing several bags of essential supplies overboard. Despite the danger and the relentless sea, Noah's determination never wavered.

Upon reaching Fair Isle, Noah and the skipper were met with hostility from the island's small population of only 48 residents. Undeterred, they began their ascent of the island's steep mountain, knowing that their prize lay on the other side. The climb was arduous, and the descent on the cliff's face was even more treacherous. At last, they reached the cavern indicated on the map, facing further dangers as they descended into its dark depths. Inside the mountain, they carefully followed the map's directions, finally arriving at the spot where they would begin digging.

For two exhausting days, Noah and the skipper toiled, their efforts finally rewarded as they uncovered Blackbeard's treasure. The sight that greeted them was beyond their wildest dreams. The cavern was filled with gold ornaments and glittering jewels, each piece more exquisite than the last. The treasure's estimated value was staggering, running into millions of dollars. Noah and the skipper could hardly believe their eyes, the culmination of Noah's lifelong quest shining brightly before them.

With the treasure found, Noah's mission was far from over. The next challenge was to transport the treasure out of the cavern and back up the mountain. The path ahead was fraught with danger, but Noah's spirit was undiminished. He looked forward to the next part of his adventure, eager to overcome whatever obstacles lay in his path and finally secure the treasure that had eluded so many before him.

 **Questions**

1. Based on the first paragraph, which word best describes Noah's feelings upon finding the map?
a) Apathetic
b) Disappointed
c) Exhilarated
d) Indifferent

2. The phrase "inconspicuous appearance and plain image" in the context of the passage suggests that the fishing boat was:
a) Luxurious and well-maintained
b) Old and worn-out
c) Highly visible and decorated
d) Modern and advanced

3. Why did Noah and the skipper choose an old fishing boat for their journey to Fair Isle?
a) It was the fastest option available.
b) It was less likely to attract attention.
c) It was the cheapest option available.
d) It was the only boat capable of making the journey.

4. Which of the following best describes the primary challenge Noah and the skipper faced during their sea journey?
a) Lack of navigation equipment
b) Hostile sea creatures
c) Adverse weather conditions
d) Mechanical failure of the boat

5. What can be inferred about the residents of Fair Isle based on their reception of Noah and the skipper?
a) They were generally friendly to visitors.
b) They were indifferent to strangers.
c) They were suspicious and unwelcoming.
d) They were eager to help treasure hunters.

6. The author describes the mountain climb and descent to the cavern in order to:
a) Emphasize the beauty of the island.
b) Highlight the dangers and challenges of the quest.
c) Describe the geological features of the island.
d) Explain why Noah chose this particular route.

7. In the context of the passage, the word "exquisite" most closely means:
a) Plain
b) Ugly
c) Beautiful
d) Common

8. Which of the following statements can be concluded from Noah's reaction upon discovering the treasure?
a) He was overwhelmed by the sheer quantity of gold and jewels.
b) He was disappointed by the small size of the treasure.
c) He was uninterested in the value of the treasure.
d) He was worried about how to transport the treasure.

9. What is the next major challenge Noah anticipates after finding the treasure?
a) Finding a buyer for the treasure
b) Transporting the treasure out of the cavern
c) Deciphering another map
d) Convincing the residents to help him

10. How does the passage exemplify the elements of a narrative adventure story?
a) It focuses on the scientific aspects of treasure hunting.
b) It describes everyday life on Fair Isle.
c) It details the historical background of Blackbeard.
d) It involves a quest with significant challenges and a valuable reward.

The Lost Treasure of Blackbeard: Writing Analysis

Now that you've read the text and responded to the questions, let's deepen our exploration by analyzing how the story is structured. This review will clarify how the narrative progresses and the techniques the author uses to engage readers, build suspense and develop characters. We will focus on how these elements work together to create an engaging story.

Below is the analysis of "The Lost Treasure of Blackbeard." As you review it, consider how the author's choices in setting, pacing, and character development might influence your own writing strategies. Think about how you can apply similar techniques in your narrative to capture your audience's attention and build a rich, engaging story.

PHASE	PURPOSE	KEY ELEMENTS and EXAMPLES
Introduction	Introduces the protagonist, Noah, and his quest to find Blackbeard's Treasure.	• **Describes Noah's long search and the moment of discovering the map.** • **Sets the scene and builds excitement for the adventure.** **Example**: "Noah had spent years searching for the fabled map of Blackbeard's Treasure."
Rising Action	Details the journey and challenges faced by Noah.	• **Vividly describes the settings such as the remote abandoned pub, the perilous journey on the old fishing boat, and the hostile island residents.** **Example**: "As they ventured into the vicious North Sea, the boat's age became painfully apparent. The journey was perilous; they battled towering waves and fierce winds, losing several bags of essential supplies overboard." • **Uses sensory details to immerse readers.** **Example**: "His heart raced with exhilaration as he unfolded the map..."

PHASE	PURPOSE	KEY ELEMENTS and EXAMPLES
Climax	Focuses on the moment of discovery of the treasure.	• **Builds suspense leading up to finding the treasure.** Example: "The climb was arduous, and the descent on the cliff's face was even more treacherous," and "For two exhausting days, Noah and the skipper toiled, their efforts finally rewarded as they uncovered Blackbeard's treasure." • **Highlights Noah's emotions and the significant details of the treasure's location.** Example: "The sight that greeted them was beyond their wildest dreams."
Falling Action	Describes the immediate aftermath of the discovery.	• **Emphasizes Noah and the Skipper's reaction.** Example: "Noah and the skipper could hardly believe their eyes, the culmination of Noah's lifelong quest shining brightly before them."
Resolution	Introduces the next phase of Noah's mission.	• **Creates anticipation for future adventures.** • **Reflects on Noah's undiminished spirit and determination.** Example: "He looked forward to the next part of his adventure, eager to overcome whatever obstacles lay in his path and finally secure the treasure that had eluded so many before him."

 Activity 2: Now that we've analyzed "The Lost Treasure of Blackbeard" and seen how a narrative is developed, let's put that knowledge to work. Choose one of the following titles and use the Story Writing Table below to help structure your narrative.

1. **The Mystery of the Whispering Cave**   2. **Escape from the Sunken City**
3. **The Race for the Lost Zodiac Stone**   4. **Journey to the Edge of the World**

Instructions:
Planning: On a separate sheet, outline your story's elements based on the Story Planning Table on page 213.
Drafting: Follow the stages in the Writing Phase Table below, to draft your narrative.
Final Submission: Include your final draft in this workbook.

Story Writing Table

PHASE	DESCRIPTION	DETAILS TO CONSIDER
1. Orientation	Introduce the setting, characters, and initial situation.	• What background information is needed? • How will you introduce the characters and setting?
2. Rising Action	Build up the tension or challenges leading to the climax.	• What events increase tension or challenge the characters? • How do these events lead up to the climax?
3. Climax	The turning point or peak of the story.	• What is the main conflict or peak event? • How does this change the course of the story?
4. Resolution	Begin resolving the conflicts introduced.	• How are the conflicts resolved? • What changes occur in the characters or setting?
5. Conclusion	Provide closure to the story.	• How will the story wrap up? • What final thoughts or messages are left with the reader?

Title: _____

Author:_____

1. Introduction
(setting, characters,
initial situation)

2. Rising Action
(tension build-up)

3. Climax
(peak or turning
point of the story)

4. Resolution
(resolving the
conflict)

5. Conclusion
(closure)

LESSON 50: Writing Descriptive Texts

Descriptive writing is a very powerful tool because it brings words to life and transports readers to places, moments or experiences through vivid language and sensory details.

Descriptive writing serves several important purposes:

- **Visualization**: Imagine reading a story where you can almost taste the salty sea air, feel a rough, sandy beach under your feet, see a bright sunset, hear the waves crashing, and smell the ocean breeze—all without leaving your chair. That's what descriptive writing does; it uses words to create a vivid picture in your mind, letting you experience places and things through your senses.

- **Engagement**: Descriptive writing is about choosing the right details that make the story or text more interesting and fun to read. It's like being a director of a movie where you get to create the scene that draws the audience in.

- **Enhancement of Narrative**: When you're telling a story, descriptive writing helps set the scene. It makes the places and people in your story feel real and important. If you're writing about a haunted house, describing the creaky floors, the chilling wind, and the faint whispers can make your story spooky and more engaging.

Descriptive writing isn't just for stories. You can use it in lots of different ways:
- **In stories** (narratives): It helps make the settings and characters come alive.
- **In explaining things** (expository writing): It can help explain things more clearly by giving concrete examples that you can picture in your mind.
- **In trying to convince someone** (persuasive writing): It can make your argument stronger by getting your readers to feel emotions or visualize situations that support your point.
- **In poems or personal journals**: It makes your writing more expressive and impactful, letting others see and feel what you do.

Activity 1: On the following page, you'll read a vivid description of the Grand Canyon. While reading:

1. Observe Sensory Details: Notice descriptions of visual, auditory, and tactile elements.
2. Identify Descriptive Techniques: Look for adjectives, metaphors, and similes that highlight the canyon's vastness and beauty.

After Reading: Complete the questions that follow.

Reading Comprehension 2: Descriptive Text

The Majestic Grand Canyon

The Grand Canyon, located in Arizona, is one of the most magnificent natural wonders of the world. Stretching over 277 miles long, up to 18 miles wide, and a mile deep, it offers breathtaking views that leave visitors in awe. The canyon's immense size and intricate landscape make it a popular destination for tourists and adventurers alike.

The walls of the Grand Canyon are adorned with layers of red rock, each telling a story of millions of years of geological history. As the sun rises and sets, the colors of the canyon walls shift dramatically, creating a spectacular display of oranges, reds, and purples. This natural phenomenon is a result of the varying mineral content in the rock layers and the angle of the sunlight.

Visitors to the Grand Canyon can explore numerous trails that wind through its rugged terrain. One of the most popular trails is the Bright Angel Trail, which offers stunning views and a challenging hike. Along the way, hikers might encounter diverse wildlife, including mule deer, California condors, and various species of reptiles.

The Colorado River, which carved out the Grand Canyon over millions of years, flows serenely at the bottom of the canyon. Rafting trips along the river provide an exhilarating way to experience the canyon's beauty from a different perspective. The river's rapids offer both thrilling adventures and moments of peaceful reflection.

Standing at the edge of the canyon, hiking its trails, or rafting its river, visitors are constantly reminded of the Grand Canyon's grandeur and the powerful forces of nature that created it.

 Questions:

1. What is the primary purpose of the passage?
a) To describe the scenic beauty and attractions of the Grand Canyon
b) To provide a historical account of the Grand Canyon
c) To explain the geological formation of the Grand Canyon
d) To discuss the wildlife in the Grand Canyon

2. In the context of the passage, what does the word "immense" most closely mean?
a) Tiny
b) Ordinary
c) Enormous
d) Unattractive

3. How does the passage describe the changing colors of the canyon walls?

a) As a result of seasonal changes

b) Due to varying weather conditions

c) Affected by human activities

d) Caused by different times of day and mineral content

4. The passage describes the Bright Angel Trail as offering "stunning views and a challenging hike." What can be inferred about the intended experience for hikers on this trail based on this description?

a) The trail is primarily for inexperienced hikers looking for an easy walk.

b) Hikers on this trail should be prepared for both beautiful scenery and a physically demanding journey.

c) The Bright Angel Trail is the only trail that offers scenic views in the Grand Canyon.

d) Visitors are likely to avoid this trail due to its challenging nature.

5. What role does the Colorado River play in the context of the passage?

a) It is the primary source of water for the area.

b) It is a feature that adds to the adventure and scenic beauty of the canyon.

c) It is a threat to the stability of the canyon.

d) It is the habitat for most of the wildlife.

6. What can be inferred about the Grand Canyon's appeal to visitors?

a) It offers a variety of activities that cater to different interests.

b) It is only popular during certain seasons.

c) It primarily attracts geologists and scientists.

d) It is a difficult place to access and visit.

7. The phrase "serenely at the bottom of the canyon" suggests that the Colorado River:

a) Flows gently and peacefully

b) Is rough and dangerous

c) Is shallow and dry

d) Flows rapidly and noisily

8. Based on the passage, what is the significance of the geological layers of the Grand Canyon?

a) They are a source of precious minerals.

b) They provide evidence of ancient civilizations.

c) They indicate volcanic activity.

d) They reveal the Earth's geological history.

Activity 2: Now that you've completed the questions, let's delve into the elements that make descriptive writing engaging and captivating.

On the following page, you will find a Descriptive Writing Template. This template will guide you in writing a vivid description of a subject of your choice. After reviewing the contents of the template, select one of the following subjects and compose a vivid and engaging description:

1. Midnight in the Enchanted Forest

2. Sunset at the Seaside Promenade

3. A Day at the Bustling City Market

4. Winter's Touch on the Sleepy Mountain Village

ELEMENT	DESCRIPTION	YOUR IDEAS and EXAMPLES
Subject	Identify the main subject of your description.	EXAMPLES: The Grand Canyon, an old city park, a bustling market)
Setting	Describe the location and time, including any relevant environmental details.	EXAMPLES: Sunrise at the Grand Canyon, a rainy afternoon in the park
Atmosphere	Convey the mood or feeling of the place.	EXAMPLES: mysterious, vibrant, peaceful
Sensory Details	Detail sensory descriptions for each sense: sight, sound, touch, taste, smell.	EXAMPLES: • **Sight**: red and purple hues of the canyon walls • **Sound**: echoes of the river • **Touch**: rough texture of the rock • **Smell**: fresh scent of the river • **Taste** (*where applicable*): crisp, tasty flavor
Figurative Language	Use metaphors, similes, personification, etc., to enrich the description.	EXAMPLES: • **Simile**: The river snaked through the canyon like a silver thread. • **Personification**: The old house groaned under the weight of the winter snow, its windows blinking against the fierce wind.
Unique Details	Include any distinctive features or details that stand out.	EXAMPLES: The unusual shape of the rocks, the color of the sky at dusk

Title: _____

Author: _____

Subject

Atmosphere

Sensory Details

Figurative Language

Unique Details

LESSON 51: Writing Expository Texts

Expository writing is a type of writing that helps you share information or explain something in a straightforward way. It's often called "informative writing" because it aims to educate the reader about a topic without including the writer's opinions.

Why Do We Use Expository Writing?

We use expository writing to explain things clearly. It can be used to detail how something works or what something is. It can also be used to instruct how to do something. In expository writing, your goal is to make your explanation easy so that the reader can follow and understand.

Where You'll See Expository Writing:

- **Essays**: Explaining a concept in a school assignment.
- **Research Papers**: Providing detailed information on a researched topic.
- **How-to Articles**: Step-by-step guides like recipes or DIY projects.
- **Reports**: Book reports, science projects, or summaries of events.
- **Instructional Texts**: Manuals or guides on using or doing something.

The table below will guide you in organizing your thoughts and ensuring that your expository texts are structured effectively.

PHASE	DESCRIPTION	EXAMPLES
1. Introduction	Introduce the topic clearly and state the objective or thesis of your text.	**Essay**: "This essay explores the impact of climate change on coral reefs." **Report**: "This report summarizes the findings of our school's annual science fair, highlighting key projects and their outcomes." **Research Paper**: "This study examines the relationship between sleep patterns and academic performance among high school students."

PHASE	DESCRIPTION	EXAMPLES
2. **Definitions** Introduce key words that will be used in your expository text and provide their definitions. Alternatively, explain key terms at their first mention.		
3. **Body**	**Detail each part of the topic, providing clear, organized information.**	**Essay:** Discuss various effects of climate change like ocean acidification and temperature rise on coral ecosystems. **Report:** Detail the most innovative projects at the fair, such as a biodegradable plastic alternative, and discuss their potential impact. **Research Paper:** Present data collected from surveys and experiments conducted over the school year, analyzing sleep duration versus grades.
4. **Use of Evidence**	**Support your points with appropriate data, examples, or quotations from sources.**	**Essay:** Use statistics from marine studies to illustrate the decline in reef health. **Report:** Include charts showing the number of participants and project categories compared to previous years. **Research Paper:** Provide graphs of sleep hours and corresponding student grades.
5. **Conclusion** Summarize the main points and the significance of the topic or findings.		

Activity 2: The reading comprehension below is an example of expository writing. It provides step-by-step instructions on how to build a simple electric circuit. When writing instructions like these, it's important to:

- List all materials needed at the start so the reader knows what they need.
- Provide detailed, step-by-step instructions that describe exactly what actions to take.
- Include any tips for success, warnings to ensure safety, and troubleshooting advice in case something doesn't work as expected.
- Clarify the purpose of each step, helping the reader understand why each action is necessary.

Reading Comprehension 3: Expository Text

How to Build a Simple Electric Circuit

Building a simple electric circuit is a fundamental experiment that helps students understand the basics of electricity and circuitry. This guide will take you through the steps needed to create a basic circuit using common materials.

Materials Needed:

1 D-cell battery
1 small light bulb (1.5V)
2 pieces of insulated wire (each about 6 inches long)
Electrical tape

Steps:

Prepare the Wires: Start by stripping about half an inch of insulation from both ends of each wire. Be careful not to cut through the wire itself.

Connect the Battery: Take one of the stripped wires and attach one end to the positive terminal of the battery. Secure it in place using electrical tape.

Attach the Light Bulb: Connect the other end of the wire to the metal base of the light bulb. Use electrical tape to ensure a firm connection.

Complete the Circuit: Take the second wire and attach one end to the negative terminal of the battery, securing it with electrical tape. Connect the other end of this wire to the side of the light bulb base. Make sure all connections are tight and secure.

Test the Circuit: Once everything is connected, the light bulb should illuminate, indicating that the circuit is complete and electricity is flowing. If the bulb does not light up, check all connections to ensure they are secure and that the wires are properly attached.

Questions:

1. What is the primary purpose of this passage?
a) To provide a historical account of electricity
b) To explain how to build a simple electric circuit
c) To discuss the benefits of using batteries
d) To compare different types of light bulbs

2. What does the word "fundamental" most closely mean in the context of the passage?
a) Complex
b) Unimportant
c) Advanced
d) Basic

3. According to the passage, what is the first step in building the electric circuit?
a) Connecting the battery
b) Testing the circuit
c) Preparing the wires
d) Attaching the light bulb

6. What role does the battery play in the electric circuit described in the passage?
a) It acts as the conductor.
b) It serves as the load.
c) It is the power source.
d) It provides insulation.

4. Why is electrical tape used in the steps described?
a) To secure the wire connections
b) To conduct electricity
c) To insulate the wires
d) To decorate the circuit

7. In the context of the passage, what does the word "secure" most closely mean?
a) Loose
b) Tight
c) Unfastened
d) Bright

5. Which of the following best describes what should be done if the light bulb does not illuminate?
a) Recheck all the connections to ensure they are secure
b) Replace the light bulb with a new one
c) Use a different type of battery
d) Increase the length of the wires

8. What can be inferred about the importance of tight and secure connections in an electric circuit?
a) They prevent the wires from overheating.
b) They help in decorating the circuit.
c) They reduce the overall cost of building the circuit.
d) They ensure that the electricity flows properly and the circuit functions correctly.

Activity 3: Now that you've read about how to build a simple electric circuit, let's delve deeper into the structure of this expository text.

Review the table below, which has been specifically adapted to the "How to Build a Simple Electric Circuit" instructions you just read. Pay close attention to how the instructions are organized and the types of information included. This analysis will help you understand the essential elements needed to ensure that readers have all the information required to successfully follow the steps.

PHASE	DESCRIPTION	DETAILS for "How to Build a Simple Electric Circuit"
Introduction	Introduce the topic and explain the purpose of the instructions.	"This guide explains the steps to build a basic electric circuit, a key experiment for understanding electricity."
Materials Needed	List all the materials required for the project.	"1 D-cell battery, 1 small light bulb (1.5V), 2 pieces of insulated wire (6 inches each), Electrical tape."
Step-by-Step Instructions	Provide detailed steps for completing the task.	The steps.
Trouble-shooting	Offer tips for solving common problems that might arise.	"If the light bulb does not illuminate, ensure all connections are tight and secure, and that wires are correctly attached to the terminals and bulb base."
Conclusion	Summarize the purpose of the project and highlight its usefulness.	"Building a simple electric circuit demonstrates basic electrical principles in action, providing foundational knowledge for more complex projects."

Activity 4: Choose one of the following titles and write an expository text about it in the space below. Ensure your explanation is clear and supported with relevant facts and details:

1. The Lifecycle of a Butterfly: From Egg to Adult
Focus: Explains the stages of a butterfly's life, describing each phase in detail.

2. Understanding the Water Cycle: Earth's Natural Recycling System
Focus: Describes the processes of evaporation, condensation, precipitation, and collection that make up the water cycle.

3. The Impact of Renewable Energy on Our Environment
Focus: Discusses various types of renewable energy sources like solar, wind, and hydroelectric power, and their benefits and challenges.

4. The History of the Internet: How It Changed Communication
Focus: Provides a chronological explanation of the development of the internet and its profound effects on global communication and information sharing.

Title: _____

Author: _____

1. Introduction
(clearly state the objective of your text)
_____
_____
_____
_____

_____ **2 - 3. Body**
_____ (provide clear and
_____ organized
_____ information and
_____ explain key terms)
_____
_____
_____
_____
_____

_____

_____

_____

4. Use of Evidence
(support your points
with data,
examples,
quotations, from
sources)

_____

_____

_____

_____

_____

_____

_____

_____

_____

_____

_____

_____

_____

5. Conclusion
(Summarize the
main points and
the significance of
the topic or
findings.)

LESSON 52: Writing Persuasive Essays

What is a Persuasive Essay?
A persuasive essay is your chance to convince someone to agree with your point of view on a particular topic. You'll use strong arguments, backed up by evidence, to persuade your readers that your stance is the best one.

Some examples of persuasive essay topics include:

- Should students have a shorter school day?
- Is it better to give than to receive?
- Should junk food be banned in schools?
- Is technology making us more alone?
- The importance of recycling to conserve the environment.

Why Write Persuasive Essays?

The purpose of writing a persuasive essay is to:

- **Convince your readers** to agree with your perspective.
- **Develop critical thinking** skills by evaluating different arguments.
- **Improve your research abilities** as you gather and present evidence.
- **Learn to write clearly and effectively** to communicate your ideas.

The Table below provides important guidelines to help you write a persuasive essay.

PHASE	DESCRIPTION	DETAILS and EXAMPLES
Introduction	Start by grabbing your reader's attention and state your main argument (thesis).	• Hook to grab attention, thesis statement, brief overview. "Imagine a world powered entirely by clean energy—this essay argues why this must become our reality."
Body Paragraph 1	Present your first supporting argument with evidence.	• Topic sentence, evidence, explanation. "Renewable energy technologies have advanced rapidly, making solar and wind energy more feasible than ever before."

PHASE	DESCRIPTION	DETAILS and EXAMPLES
Body Paragraph 2	Provide a second argument or address a common counterargument to show you've thought of multiple sides.	• Topic sentence, further evidence, explanation. "Many worry about the reliability of renewable energy, yet modern advancements in energy storage are overcoming these challenges."
Body Paragraph 3	Discuss a possible objection to your argument and refute* it with evidence. *Refute - To prove that something is wrong or false by using evidence or arguments.*	• Counterargument, explanation. "Opponents claim renewable energy is too costly, but long-term savings on utility bills actually make it more economical than traditional fuels."
Conclusion	Wrap up by summarizing your arguments and reinforcing your thesis with a powerful closing statement.	• Restate thesis, summarize arguments, counterarguments, "Switching to renewable energy isn't just an environmental necessity but an economic opportunity we must seize for a sustainable future."

Activity 1: On the following page, you'll read a persuasive essay on the importance of a balanced diet.

While Reading:
- **Identify the Thesis:** Note the main point the author is trying to convince you of.
- **Spot Main Arguments:** Look for key arguments that support the thesis.
- **Detect Counterarguments:** Observe if the author addresses any opposing views and how they refute them.

After Reading:

Answer the Questions: These will help you reflect on the effectiveness of the arguments and understand the structure of a persuasive essay.

Reading Comprehension 4: Persuasive Essay

The Importance of a Balanced Diet

A balanced diet is crucial for maintaining good health and well-being. It provides the body with essential nutrients, supports immune function, and helps prevent chronic diseases. In this essay, I will argue why everyone should prioritize a balanced diet.

Firstly, a balanced diet includes a variety of foods that supply the necessary vitamins, minerals, and other nutrients the body needs to function properly. Fruits and vegetables, for example, are rich in vitamins and antioxidants that boost the immune system and help the body fight off infections. Whole grains and proteins provide energy and support muscle growth and repair.

Secondly, consuming a balanced diet can prevent various health issues. Diets high in processed foods, sugars, and unhealthy fats are linked to obesity, diabetes, and heart disease. By choosing nutritious foods, individuals can reduce their risk of developing these conditions. For instance, incorporating more fiber-rich foods, such as legumes and whole grains, can improve digestive health and lower cholesterol levels.

Moreover, a balanced diet contributes to better mental health. Studies have shown that there is a connection between diet and mood. Eating a variety of nutrient-dense foods can reduce the risk of depression and anxiety. Omega-3 fatty acids found in fish, nuts, and seeds are known to support brain health and cognitive function.

In conclusion, prioritizing a balanced diet is essential for overall health. It not only provides the necessary nutrients for bodily functions but also helps prevent chronic diseases and supports mental well-being. By making informed food choices and avoiding processed foods, individuals can lead healthier and happier lives.

 **Questions:**

1. What is the primary purpose of the essay?
a) To compare different types of diets
b) To discuss the role of exercise in maintaining health
c) To describe the effects of processed foods
d) To explain the benefits of a balanced diet

2. In the context of the essay, what does the word "crucial" most closely mean?
a) Essential
b) Unnecessary
c) Optional
d) Difficult

3. What role do fruits and vegetables play in maintaining health, according to the essay?
a) They predominantly serve as the body's source of proteins.
b) They act as the sole providers of necessary dietary components.
c) Their rich content of vitamins and antioxidants helps enhance immune defense.
d) They replace all other necessary food groups.

4. In the context of the essay, how do whole grains contribute to one's health?
a) They are known for their anti-inflammatory properties.
b) They aid in muscle maintenance.
c) They are primarily valued for their high antioxidant content.
d) They are recognized for their high omega-3 fatty acid content.

5. Which of the following best describes the connection between diet and mental health discussed in the essay?
a) Diet has no impact on mental health.
b) Eating nutrient-dense foods can improve mood and reduce the risk of depression and anxiety.
c) Only sugary foods can boost mental health.
d) Processed foods are beneficial for mental health.

6. What can be inferred about the author's view on processed foods?
a) They are beneficial for health.
b) They have no effect on health.
c) They are essential for a balanced diet.
d) They should be avoided for better health.

7. In the context of the essay, what is the significance of Omega-3 fatty acids?
a) They enhance mental acuity and support neurological health.
b) They boost the immune system.
c) They provide energy and support muscle growth.
d) They improve digestive health and lower cholesterol levels.

8. Which of the following best summarizes the conclusion of the essay?
a) Prioritizing a diet high in protein is essential for muscle growth and overall health.
b) Consuming dairy products is the key to achieving a balanced diet and strong bones.
c) A diet rich in various nutrients is vital for maintaining good health and preventing deficiencies.
d) Eliminating fats and sugars completely from one's diet ensures optimal health.

Activity 2: Now that we've explored the characteristics of persuasive writing, it's time to put what you've learned into practice. Choose one of the following topics and write a persuasive essay in the space provided below:

1. Should Musicians and Actors Be Considered Role Models?

2. Is Participation in Sports Essential for Teen Development?

3. The Impact of Social Media on Teenagers: More Harmful Than Helpful?

4. Should Video Games Be Considered a Sport?

Title: _____

Author:_____

Introduction 1. What interesting fact or statement can you use to grab attention? 2. What is your position on the topic? 3. Why should the reader care about this issue?	
Body Paragraph 1 1. What is your strongest argument? 2. What evidence supports this argument? 3. How does this support your thesis?	
Body Paragraph 2 1. What is another compelling argument for your thesis? 2. What is a common opposition argument, and how can you refute it?	
Body Paragraph 2 1. What might opponents say against your thesis? 2. How can you show that these objections are unfounded or less important than your points?	
Conclusion How can you summarize your arguments and final thoughts briefly?	

LESSON 53: Writing a Report

What is a Report?

Think of a report as a fact-finding mission where your job is to gather information, analyze it, and then share it with others in a very organized way. Reports are frequently used in schools, businesses, and science projects to help people make decisions or understand topics better.

The Purpose of a Report

Reports are ideal for:
- **Informing**: Sharing important facts and findings with others.
- **Analyzing**: Examining closely what the information means.
- **Recommending**: Suggesting what should be done based on what you've learned.

Differences Between Reports and Other Writing:

- **Structure**: Reports are organized into specific sections. You typically see parts labeled as "Methodology" where the methods of research are explained, "Findings" where the results are shown, and "Recommendations" where advice based on the findings is given.
- **Language**: The language used in reports is straightforward and factual. It focuses on delivering information clearly and accurately, without using elaborate or flowery language.
- **Visuals**: Reports often include charts, graphs, and tables. These visuals help present data in a clear way, making it easier to understand complex information.

Similarities to Other Writing:

- **Purpose**: Like expository essays, reports are designed to inform or explain. They provide detailed information on a specific topic.
- **Organization**: Reports have a clear structure with an introduction that sets up the topic, a body that delves into the details, and a conclusion that wraps up the discussion, similar to many other essays.
- **Evidence**: Just as in persuasive and expository essays, where supporting your points with evidence is crucial, reports also require solid evidence to back up the conclusions drawn from the data.

Reading Comprehension 5: Report

Candy Consumption Among Teenagers in Springfield, USA

Abstract

This report analyzes the patterns of candy consumption among teenagers in Springfield, focusing on the types and quantities of candy consumed monthly. The findings aim to provide insights for local health initiatives targeted at promoting healthier eating habits among adolescents.

Introduction

Candy consumption is a prevalent habit among teenagers, often linked to increased risks of dental issues and other health problems. This study seeks to quantify candy consumption in Springfield to inform potential health policy adjustments.

Methodology

Data was collected from a survey conducted among 300 teenagers aged 13-18 in Springfield, using self-reported measures of candy consumption over the past month. The survey included various types of candy, such as chocolate, hard candies, gummies, and licorice.

Findings

The survey revealed that 75% of teenagers consume candy at least twice a week. The average monthly candy intake per teenager was found to be approximately 500 grams.

Analysis

The high frequency and quantity of candy consumption suggest a significant trend among local teenagers. Increased consumption of high-sugar products like candy is associated with higher risks of obesity and dental problems.

Conclusion

Teenagers in Springfield consume a substantial amount of candy, which may contribute to health complications. There is a need for programs that encourage healthier dietary choices among youth.

Recommendations

- Implement educational programs in schools to promote healthier eating habits.
- Increase the availability of healthier snack alternatives in school cafeterias.
- Conduct regular health and nutrition workshops for students and parents.

| Chart: Average Monthly Candy Consumption by Type | |
Type of Candy	Average Consumption (grams)
Chocolate	200
Hard Candies	150
Gummies	100
Licorice	50

Questions:

1. What is the primary focus of this report?

a) The health implications of candy consumption
b) The types of candy preferred by teenagers in Springfield
c) Candy consumption patterns among teenagers in Springfield
d) Dental health among teenagers in Springfield

2. Based on the findings, which statement best describes the frequency of candy consumption among Springfield teenagers?

a) The majority consume candy occasionally, around once a month.
b) Most teenagers consume candy multiple times throughout the week.
c) Candy is consumed on a daily basis by nearly all teenagers.
d) Candy consumption is infrequent among the majority of teenagers.

3. What methodology was used to gather data for the report?

a) Self-reported surveys
b) Physical health assessments
c) Interviews with parents
d) Observation

4. Based on the chart, how many grams of candy, excluding chocolate, are consumed on average per month by teenagers in Springfield?

a) 200 grams
b) 250 grams
c) 300 grams
d) 350 grams

5. According to the report, which statement most accurately describes the risks associated with high candy consumption among teenagers in Springfield?

a) Higher risks of obesity.
b) Higher risks of dental problems.
c) Higher risks of health problems in general.
d) Higher risks of obesity and dental problems.

6. Which section of the report provides a visual summary of the data?

a) The Chart
b) The Conclusion
c) The Abstract
d) The Recommendations

Now that you've learned about the key features and purposes of writing a report, let's get hands-on! It's time to create a fun and engaging survey that will form the foundation for your report. Start by selecting one of the titles provided. Once you have your topic, follow the guidelines on the next page to design your survey. This will gather the data you need to write an insightful report.

1. **Which Superpower Do Our Classmates Wish They Had?**

2. **Favorite School Lunches: What Tops the Charts?**

Guidelines for Preparing your Survey

1. Collecting Data
It's time to get your questions out there and collect some answers!

Step 1: Choose Your Survey Format
- You can either print your survey questions on paper and hand them out in class or during lunch, or
- Create a digital version using Google Forms, which is easy to share via email or social media.

Here are Some Survey Questions to Get You Started:

Title 1: Which Superpower Do Our Classmates Wish They Had?
1. Which superpower would you choose? Choose from Flying, Invisibility, Super Strength, Telepathy, or something else you might prefer!
2. Why would you choose this superpower? Share your reasons in a few sentences.
3. How often would this superpower be useful to you? Would it be every day, once a week, occasionally, or rarely?
4. Who is your favorite superhero with this power and why? Tell us who inspires you!

Title 2: Favorite School Lunches: What Tops the Charts?
1. What's your favorite school lunch? Is it pizza, burgers, tacos, salad, or something else?
2. How would you rate our school lunches from 1 (poor) to 5 (excellent)?
3. What kind of meal would you love to see added to our menu? Maybe vegetarian, gluten-free, international dishes, or healthier snacks?
4. If you could change one thing about our lunches, what would it be?

2. Analyzing Your Data

Step 1: Summarize the Findings
- **Compile Responses:** Gather and organize the responses for each question.
- **Identify Trends:** Determine the most and least popular choices from the survey data.

Step 2: Analyze the Findings
- **Group Responses:** Categorize the reasons provided by classmates for their choices.
- **Discover Themes:** Identify common themes or notable insights from the grouped reasons.

Step 3: Write Your Report and Present It
- **Draft Your Report:** Use the structure and elements from Reading Comprehension 5 as a model for your report.
- **Presentation:** Prepare to present your findings clearly and concisely to your classmates, incorporating visuals or graphics to enhance understanding and engagement.

LESSON 54: Personal Writing and Formal Writing

Have you ever wondered why you talk differently to your friends than you do in a classroom presentation? In this lesson, we're going to explore the differences between personal writing, like journal entries and letters to friends, and formal writing, which you use in school essays or official emails.

What is Personal Writing?

Personal writing, also referred to as "informal writing," is any writing that you do mainly for yourself or people you know well. It can be fun and free-form, and it includes:

- Diaries or journals
- Personal letters or emails
- Messages to friends and family

Characteristics of Personal Writing:

- Conversational Tone: It's like chatting with a friend.
- Slang and Everyday Language: You can be informal and use phrases and words you use every day.
- Emotions and Opinions: Feel free to express how you feel and what you think.

What is Formal Writing?

Formal writing is more serious and is used when you need to be professional. You use it for:

- School Assignments: Like essays or big projects where you need clear, structured writing without slang.
- Official Letters: Such as those to principals or other professionals to make a good impression.
- Professional Emails: When emailing teachers or professionals, showing respect and seriousness.

Key Differences between Personal and Formal Writing:

- Tone: Formal writing keeps emotions in check, aiming for a calm and collected approach.
- Language: Every word matters in formal writing. Avoid slang and choose words that are clear and precise.
- Focus on Facts: Stick to facts and proven information, leaving out personal stories unless they are relevant to the topic.

In the following activities, you will read two passages: the first is a set of journal entries, which serve as a model for personal (informal) writing, and the second is a legal letter, exemplifying formal writing.

While reading: Note the tone and language used in each passage.

After reading: Answer the questions provided after each passage.

Reading Comprehension 6: Journal Entries

A Week in the Life of a Student

Monday, July 15

Today was the first day of summer camp, and I was both excited and nervous. We started with an icebreaker activity to get to know each other. I met some interesting people, including my new friend, Sam. We spent the afternoon working on a group project about renewable energy sources. It was fascinating to learn about solar panels and wind turbines.

Tuesday, July 16

I woke up early for a nature hike organized by the camp counselors. The trail was beautiful, filled with wildflowers and tall trees. Along the way, we spotted various birds and even a deer. Our guide explained the importance of preserving natural habitats, which made me think about how I can contribute to environmental conservation.

Wednesday, July 17

Today was all about science experiments. We conducted an experiment to create a homemade volcano using baking soda and vinegar. It was amazing to see the chemical reaction in action. Later, we had a workshop on coding, which was a bit challenging but incredibly rewarding when I finally got my code to work.

Thursday, July 18

We had a sports day, and I participated in several events, including a relay race and tug-of-war. My team didn't win, but we had a lot of fun and learned the value of teamwork and sportsmanship. In the evening, we gathered around a campfire, roasted marshmallows, and shared stories. It was the perfect way to end the day.

Friday, July 19

Our final day at camp was bittersweet. We presented our group projects to the rest of the camp. Our renewable energy project received positive feedback, and I felt proud of what we accomplished. We exchanged contact information to stay in touch. As I packed my things, I reflected on the amazing experiences and friendships I made this week.

1. What does the word "fascinating" most nearly mean as used in the sentence "It was fascinating to learn about solar panels and wind turbines"?
a) Informative
b) Enjoyable
c) Captivating
d) Surprising

2. Based on the journal entries, what was the primary purpose of the nature hike organized by the camp counselors?
a) To observe and appreciate the natural environment
b) To reflect about how to contribute to environmental conservation
c) To observe wildflowers and tall trees
d) To observe birds in their natural habitat

3. Which sentence from the journal entry supports the idea that the narrator learned about teamwork during camp?
a) "We spent the afternoon working on a group project about renewable energy sources."
b) "My team didn't win, but we had a lot of fun and learned the value of teamwork and sportsmanship."
c) "Later, we had a workshop on coding, which was a bit challenging but incredibly rewarding when I finally got my code to work."
d) "Our final day at camp was bittersweet."

4. What was the outcome of the sports day for the writer's team on Thursday?
a) They won several events.
b) They learned about teamwork and sportsmanship despite not winning.
c) They didn't participate in any events.
d) They were disappointed by their performance.

5. Based on the diary entry for Wednesday, what can be inferred about the writer's experience with coding?
a) The writer found coding easy and straightforward.
b) The writer gave up on coding due to its difficulty.
c) The writer was uninterested in coding.
d) The writer struggled initially.

6. What is the meaning of the word "bittersweet" as used in the entry for Friday?
a) Tasting both bitter and sweet
b) Being both excited and angry
c) Being uncertain and confused
d) Feeling happy and sad at the same time

7. Which event on Thursday was described as "the perfect way to end the day"?
a) The relay race
b) The coding workshop
c) The campfire gathering
d) The group project presentation

8. Which of the following best describes the overall tone of the journal entries?
a) Appreciative
b) Bittersweet
c) Driven
d) Indifferent

Reading Comprehension 7: Formal Letter

Trademark Infringement Notice

Johnathan E. Clark, Esq.
Clark & Associates Legal Firm
1200 Legal Gateway Plaza
San Francisco, CA 94107
Email: j.clark@clarkassociates.com
Phone: (415) 555-0198
July 28, 2024

Mr. Thomas H. Bradley
CEO, GlobalTech Innovations Corp.
2000 Innovation Drive
San Jose, CA 95050

Dear Mr. Bradley,

Re: Trademark Infringement Notice

I am writing to you on behalf of our client, Premier Designs Ltd., concerning a critical issue that has recently come to our attention. It has been observed that GlobalTech Innovations Corp. has been utilizing a trademark that is unmistakably similar to our client's registered trademark, specifically the stylized logo used in conjunction with their consumer electronics product line. This use constitutes a direct infringement of our client's intellectual property rights.

Our client is the exclusive holder of this trademark, substantiated by federal registration with the United States Patent and Trademark Office (Registration No. 7891234). The unauthorized usage of this trademark has not only caused confusion among consumers but has also diluted the distinctive quality of our client's well-established brand.

Under Section 32(1) of the Lanham Act, your company's actions are considered an infringement involving the use in commerce of a reproduction, counterfeit, copy, or colorable imitation of a registered mark. This usage is connected with the sale, distribution, or advertising of goods or services, which is likely to cause confusion or deception among consumers. Therefore, we formally request that GlobalTech Innovations Corp. immediately cease and desist from any further use of the trademark in question.

Should GlobalTech Innovations Corp. fail to discontinue these infringing activities within ten (10) business days from the date of this letter, please be informed that our client is prepared to initiate legal proceedings to enforce its rights. This includes seeking an injunction to prevent further violations and pursuing claims for monetary damages, which may encompass both actual and statutory damages.

We expect a response to this notice on or before August 8, 2024, and appreciate your cooperation in resolving this matter promptly. Please address your correspondence and any queries to my attention at the contact details provided above.

Thank you for your immediate attention to this pressing issue.

Sincerely,
Johnathan E. Clark, Esq.
Clark & Associates Legal Firm

 Questions:

1. What rationale does Johnathan E. Clark provide for the necessity of the cease and desist action?
a) To protect the client's exclusive rights and investment in their trademark.
b) To comply with international trading standards.
c) To encourage healthy competition among industry players.
d) To safeguard the public from misleading advertising.

2. **How does the trademark infringement allegedly affect Premier Designs Ltd.?**
a) It compromises their financial stability due to lost sales.
b) It disrupts their operational processes.
c) It leads to potential legal penalties from regulatory bodies.
d) It undermines the uniqueness of their brand in the market.

3. What consequence does Johnathan E. Clark warn of if compliance is not met within the specified period?
a) Financial compensation will be sought for past infringements.
b) Further use of the trademark by GlobalTech will be sanctioned.
c) Legal measures will be taken to prevent future misuse.
d) Collaboration between both companies will be reconsidered.

4. What does the letter explicitly request from Mr. Bradley within ten business days?
a) An official retraction of all products bearing the contested trademark.
b) A proposal for settlement to avoid court proceedings.
c) Ceasing the disputed use of the trademark.
d) Confirmation of receipt and understanding of the legal notice.

5. Writing Structure and Language Questions: Which aspect of the letter's structure enhances its formal nature?
a) The alignment of text and the font used in the letter.
b) The inclusion of a specific legal statute as a foundational argument.
c) The detailed recounting of the client's trademark registration history.
d) The brief introduction and immediate transition to legal matters.

6. **Why is precise language particularly crucial in this legal communication?**
a) It decorates the content to appear more authoritative.
b) It provides an educational insight into legal terminology for the recipient.
c) It demonstrates the lawyer's command over legal discourse.
d) It minimizes the risk of misinterpretation and potential legal loopholes.

Comparing and Contrasting Informal and Formal Writing

Now that you have read the two passages and answered the questions, we will explore the tone, language, and structure of each. This will help us highlight the differences between the informal journal entries and the formal legal letter.

1. **Tone**:
   - Journal Entries (informal): The tone is friendly and personal, capturing the excitement and reflections of daily activities at summer camp.
   - Legal Letter (formal): The tone is professional and authoritative, addressing a serious issue of trademark infringement with urgency.
2. **Language**:
   - Journal Entries: Casual and conversational, using everyday language that includes expressions of feelings and personal observations.
   - Legal Letter: Precise and technical, employing specific legal terms and formal structures to clearly outline the legal complaint and demands.
3. **Structure**:
   - Journal Entries: Organized chronologically, each entry marks a new day with descriptions of events and personal thoughts, flowing like a diary.
   - Legal Letter: Structured with a formal opening, a detailed body explaining the legal issue, and a closing that includes a direct demand for action.

Now that you've explored the differences between formal and informal writing, it's your turn to practice what you've learned. Using the informal style demonstrated in the journal entries, create your own journal entry based on one of the following prompts:

1. **A Day I Will Never Forget. Describe an unforgettable experience and how it impacted you.**
2. **My Favorite Hobby. Explain what your hobby is, why you enjoy it, and how you got started.**
3. **The Best Vacation Ever. Share details about the best vacation you've ever had and what made it so special.**
4. **A Letter to My Future Self. Write a letter to your future self, sharing your hopes and dreams.**

My Daily Journal

Date: _____

LESSON 55: Writing a Dialogue

What is Dialogue?
Dialogue is the written conversational exchange between two or more characters. It's a powerful tool in both fiction and nonfiction writing that helps bring characters to life and advance the plot.

Dialogue refers to the words spoken by characters in a story or a play. It's one of the key elements that writers use to develop characters and move the story forward. In scripts and plays, dialogue is the main component that actors perform.

The Purpose of Dialogue in Writing:
- Character Development: Dialogue reveals a lot about a character's personality, background, and relationships through what they say and how they say it.
- Advancing the Plot: Conversations between characters can introduce new plot points or resolve conflicts.
- Building Tension: Writers often use dialogue to build suspense and tension within their stories.
- Enhancing Realism: Good dialogue can make characters and scenes feel real and relatable, helping readers connect with the text on a deeper level.

The Structure of Dialogue:
- Tags and Beats: Dialogue tags (e.g., said, asked) show who is speaking. Action beats give readers extra information about what the character is doing while speaking.
- Punctuation: Proper punctuation is crucial in dialogue. Commas, periods, question marks, and exclamation points are placed inside the quotation marks if they are part of the spoken sentence.
- Paragraphs: A new paragraph begins every time a different character starts speaking. This helps keep the conversation clear and easy to follow.

How to Write Effective Dialogue:
- Keep It Natural: Write dialogue that sounds believable and natural for the characters. Avoid overly formal language unless it suits the character.
- Be Concise: Dialogue should be brief and impactful. It's not the place for long-winded speeches (unless it's essential to the character).
- Use Contractions: People often use contractions (can't, won't, I'm) in everyday speech. Including them can make your dialogue sound more authentic.
- Listen to How People Talk: Paying attention to real conversations can help you understand how to write dialogue that sounds realistic.

Activity 1: In the upcoming activity, read the dialogue between two schoolmates, paying attention to the structure and natural flow of the conversation. After reading, answer the questions that follow.

Reading Comprehension 8: Dialogue

School Struggles

Jayden: Hey William, how's everything going with your new classes?

William: It's overwhelming, to be honest. The homework load has doubled since last year, and I barely have time for anything else.

Jayden: I get that. I've been staying up late just to keep up with math and science. It feels like there's this huge expectation to always be on top of everything.

William: Exactly, and on top of that, everyone seems to be joining so many clubs and sports. I feel like if I don't, I'll be left out.

Jayden: That's the peer pressure kicking in. I joined the chess club and the swimming team because my friends did. But honestly, I don't enjoy swimming that much.

William: It's tricky, right? We're supposed to balance schoolwork, hobbies, and our social lives, but it's like everything demands to be a priority.

Jayden: And it's not just the activities. Even choosing subjects feels like a huge deal. Everyone says STEM subjects are crucial for a good career, but what if I prefer creative writing?

William: I hear you. My sister told me it's important to follow what actually interests you, not just what looks good on paper. Maybe we need to think more about what makes us happy rather than what impresses others.

Jayden: That's a good point. Maybe I should give more thought to what I really enjoy studying. How do you handle all these decisions?

William: Taking it one day at a time, and talking helps. Like now, discussing it makes it a bit easier to manage.

Jayden: True, talking does help. Let's keep checking in with each other, maybe share tips on managing stress?

William: Sounds like a plan. Thanks, Jayden.

1. What underlying reason might Jayden have for participating in extracurricular activities, according to the dialogue?
a) To explore diverse interests and hobbies.
b) To enhance his college applications.
c) To improve his academic performance.
d) Due to the influence of his peers.

2. Which excerpt from the dialogue best illustrates William's struggle with the increased academic demands?
a) "We're supposed to balance schoolwork, hobbies, and our social lives."
b) "It feels like there's this huge expectation to always be on top of everything."
c) "The homework load has doubled since last year, and I barely have time for anything else."
d) "I've been staying up late just to keep up with math and science."

3. What does William imply by describing his situation as "overwhelming" in the context of their discussion?
a) He finds the increased academic workload unmanageable.
b) He is indifferent to the challenges posed by school.
c) He sees the workload as a positive challenge.
d) He is unsure about his ability to meet expectations.

4. How does William's perspective on extracurricular activities reflect broader societal pressures?
a) He views them as crucial for social integration.
b) He believes they are optional and primarily for personal growth.
c) He feels compelled to participate due to external expectations.
d) He participates solely for personal enjoyment.

5. What dialogue suggests Jayden is reconsidering his approach to extracurricular activities?
a) "But honestly, I don't enjoy swimming that much."
b) "Let's keep checking in with each other, maybe share tips on managing stress?"
c) "It's tricky, right? We're supposed to balance schoolwork, hobbies, and our social lives."
d) "Maybe I should give more thought to what I really enjoy studying."

6. In Jayden's statement about choosing subjects being a "huge deal," what is implied about his feelings towards making such decisions?
a) He considers it a trivial and unimportant choice.
b) He views it as a critical and potentially overwhelming decision.
c) He is excited and enthusiastic about the options available.
d) He feels detached and uninterested in the decision-making process.

7. Based on their conversation, how do Jayden and William typically manage the pressures of school and extracurricular activities?
a) By minimizing their involvement in stressful activities.
b) By actively seeking guidance from peers and older siblings.
c) Through mutual support and sharing coping strategies.
d) By conforming strictly to what is popular among their peers.

Activity 2: Choose one of the following titles and write a dialogue that reflects the given scenario. Focus on creating realistic exchanges that reveal the characters' perspectives and emotions.

1. Future Tech in Our Classroom. Two classmates imagine how technology will change school life in ten years.

2. The New School Club. Two students plan the activities for a new club they want to start.

3. Science Fair Partners. Two classmates discuss their ideas and plan their project for the upcoming science fair.

4. The Talent Show Tryouts. Two friends talk about their preparations and nerves for the school talent show auditions.

Title: _____

_____: _____

_____: _____

_____: _____

_____: _____

_____: _____

_____: _____

_____: _____

_____: _____

_____: _____

LESSON 56: Writing an Opinion Article

 A newspaper opinion article, often called an op-ed, is a piece where the writer expresses their personal views and arguments about a specific issue. These articles aim to persuade readers to see a topic from the writer's perspective.

Here are some important characteristics to keep in mind:

- **Clear Thesis:** Every great opinion article starts with a clear statement of the writer's main argument or position. This is your thesis, and it guides everything you write, explaining to your readers what you believe and why.
- **Strong Supporting Arguments:** To persuade your readers, you need to support your thesis with strong, logical arguments. Use facts, statistics, quotes from experts, and other evidence to back up your points.
- **Personal Voice and Style:** Opinion articles allow you to express your personality in your writing. Your voice can be passionate, humorous, or earnest, depending on the topic and your style. This personal touch helps connect with your readers and makes your argument more compelling.
- **Address Counterarguments:** A good opinion article also considers opposing views. By addressing counterarguments, you can strengthen your own position by showing that you have thought about different sides of the issue.
- **Conclusion with a Call to Action:** End your article by summarizing your main points and encouraging your readers to think, feel, or act differently based on your argument. This is your chance to leave a lasting impression.

 **Activity 1: Now that you understand what makes a newspaper opinion article effective, you'll read an example titled "The Debate Over School Uniforms: Necessary Discipline or Restrictive Practice?" As you read, notice how the writer presents their arguments and engages with the topic. After reading, answer the questions that follow.**

Reading Comprehension 9: Newspaper Opinion Article

The Debate Over School Uniforms: Necessary Discipline or Restrictive Practice?

The debate over whether school uniforms should be mandatory in public schools has been a contentious issue for years. Proponents argue that uniforms promote discipline, reduce distractions, and create a sense of equality among students. Opponents, however, believe that uniforms suppress individuality and impose unnecessary restrictions on students' freedom of expression.

As an educator with over twenty years of experience, I have seen firsthand the impact of school uniforms on the learning environment. In schools where uniforms are required, there is a noticeable difference in student behavior. Uniforms seem to foster a sense of seriousness and purpose, leading to fewer disruptions and more focus on academics. This is not just my personal observation but a sentiment echoed by many of my colleagues.

Moreover, uniforms can alleviate the social pressures associated with fashion and economic disparities. When students wear the same attire, there is less opportunity for bullying based on clothing choices. This creates a more inclusive environment where students can concentrate on their studies rather than their appearance.

However, it's essential to consider the arguments of those who oppose school uniforms. Critics argue that uniforms stifle creativity and self-expression, which are crucial aspects of adolescent development. In a society that values individuality, forcing students to conform to a standard dress code may hinder their ability to develop a unique sense of self.

Additionally, the financial burden of purchasing uniforms can be significant for some families, particularly those with multiple children. Although uniforms are intended to level the playing field, they can inadvertently create economic strain, exacerbating the very inequalities they aim to address.

In conclusion, the question of whether school uniforms should be mandatory is complex and multifaceted. While uniforms can promote discipline and reduce social pressures, they may also suppress individuality and impose financial burdens. As with many educational policies, the key lies in finding a balance that considers the diverse needs and perspectives of all students.

 **Questions:**

1. What is the primary purpose of the article?
a) To describe the history of school uniforms
b) To argue in favor of school uniforms
c) To report on a new school uniform policy
d) To present both sides of the debate over school uniforms

2. Which sentence is more formal?
a) "Uniforms seem to foster a sense of seriousness and purpose, leading to fewer disruptions and more focus on academics."
b) "Critics argue that uniforms stifle creativity and self-expression, which are crucial aspects of adolescent development."

3. What is the tone of the article?
a) Neutral and balanced
b) Humorous and light-hearted
c) Angry and confrontational
d) Sympathetic and emotional

4. What does the figure of speech "level the playing field" most closely mean in the context of the article?
a) Ensure all students play sports equally
b) Make the school environment fair and equal for all students
c) Require students to wear the same uniforms
d) Flatten the school grounds

5. What can be inferred about the author's stance on school uniforms?
a) The author is strongly against school uniforms.
b) The author is strongly in favor of school uniforms.
c) The author sees both benefits and drawbacks to school uniforms.
d) The author believes uniforms should only be used in private schools.

 Activity 2: Select one of the titles below and write your opinion article in the template provided. This activity will help you practice your persuasive writing skills by allowing you to express your views on current issues.

1. The Value of Art and Music Education in Schools

2. Should Students Have a Say in Curriculum Design

3. Green Schools: Should Environmental Education Be Mandatory?

4. The Role of Field Trips in Education: Are They Worth the Effort?

Introduction

- Hook: (Start with an interesting statement or question to grab the reader's attention.)
- Thesis Statement: (Clearly state your main argument or position on the topic.)
- Background Information: (Provide a brief overview of the issue or topic being discussed.)

Body Paragraph 1

- Main Argument: (State your first supporting point.)
- Evidence: (Include facts, statistics, quotes, or examples that support this point.)
- Explanation: (Explain how this evidence supports your thesis.)

Body Paragraph 2

- Main Argument: (State your second supporting point.)
- Evidence: (Provide supporting details as above.)
- Explanation: (Link back to your thesis.)

Body Paragraph 2

- Counterargument: (Acknowledge a common opposition view to your argument.)
- Rebuttal: (Refute the counterargument with evidence and reasoning.)

Conclusion

- Summary of your thesis and arguments.
- Call to Action: (Prompt readers to think, feel, or act on the issue.)

LESSON 57: Research Skills

As you continue your journey through school and beyond, knowing how to gather, evaluate, and use information effectively will be extremely important. Good research skills are essential when working on a school project, writing an essay, or simply exploring the world. They help you find answers and make informed decisions.

In this lesson, we'll explore the fundamental elements of conducting research, laying a good foundation as you advance from middle school to high school.

Understanding Your Topic
Every good research project starts with a clear thesis question. What do you need to find out? Understand your assignment and the main and subsidiary questions you need to answer. This focus prevents drifting off-topic.

Finding Reliable Sources
Once you know the questions you're answering, choose your sources carefully. Spend time reading to decide which sources are trustworthy. Ask: Who is the author? When was this published? Is this source biased? Stick to books, academic journals, and reputable websites, and be cautious with unverified internet content.

Taking Effective Notes
With reliable sources identified, take detailed notes. Organize your notes well to simplify the writing process later. Once you've gathered sufficient information, you can start drafting your paper.

Writing a Draft
Focus on developing your ideas in the first draft rather than writing perfectly. Present your thesis question, explore what other authors have said about it, and discuss arguments and counterarguments. After completing your draft, you can start refining it.

Plagiarism and Citing Sources
Always credit the original authors for their ideas, arguments, or concepts by citing your sources. Whether you use MLA, APA, or Chicago style, proper citation is crucial to avoid plagiarism.

Revising Your Work
Review and revise your drafts to enhance your arguments and ensure clarity. Check that all information is accurately cited.

Activity 1: In this activity, you will read a researched biography that provides information about the life of Nikola Tesla. After reading, answer the questions that follow.

Reading Comprehension 10: Biography

The Life of Nikola Tesla

Nikola Tesla was a brilliant inventor and engineer whose contributions to the field of electrical engineering revolutionized the world. Born on July 10, 1856, in Smiljan, Croatia, Tesla displayed an early aptitude for mathematics and science. He attended the Austrian Polytechnic in Graz and later studied at the University of Prague.

Tesla's most notable work involved the development of alternating current (AC) electrical systems. His innovations in AC technology provided a more efficient method for transmitting electricity over long distances compared to the direct current (DC) systems championed by Thomas Edison. Tesla's AC system became the standard for electrical power transmission and is still in use today.

In addition to his work on AC systems, Tesla made significant contributions to the development of wireless communication. He envisioned a world where information could be transmitted without wires, a concept that laid the groundwork for modern wireless technology. Tesla's experiments with radio waves and electromagnetic fields were groundbreaking, although he faced many challenges and setbacks throughout his career.

Tesla was also known for his eccentric personality and imaginative ideas. He claimed to have invented a "death ray" and a machine capable of generating earthquakes, although these claims were never substantiated. Despite his many successes, Tesla struggled financially and spent his later years living in relative obscurity.

Nikola Tesla passed away on January 7, 1943, in New York City. Although he did not achieve the same level of fame as some of his contemporaries during his lifetime, his contributions to science and technology have been widely recognized and celebrated posthumously. Today, Tesla is remembered as a visionary whose innovations continue to impact our daily lives.

 Questions:

1. What was Tesla's most notable contribution to electrical engineering?
a) Direct current systems
b) Wireless communication
c) Alternating current systems
d) Nuclear power

2. In the context of the passage, what does the word "revolutionized" most closely mean?
a) Transformed
b) Rejected
c) Simplified
d) Complicated

3. Which of the following best describes Tesla's vision for the future of communication?
a) Communication through wires
b) Face-to-face communication
c) Wireless communication
d) Written communication

4. What does the passage suggest about Tesla's claims of inventing a "death ray" and an earthquake machine?
a) They were widely accepted.
b) They were never proven.
c) They were put to practical use.
d) They were ignored by everyone.

5. How did Tesla's financial situation impact his later years?
a) He became very wealthy.
b) He continued to invent and innovate without any issues.
c) He received financial support from the government.
d) He faced economic hardships.

6. Which of the following can be inferred about Tesla's recognition during his lifetime?
a) He was more famous than Thomas Edison.
b) He achieved significant fame and wealth.
c) He was not as famous as some of his contemporaries.
d) He was completely unknown.

7. What does the passage imply about the lasting impact of Tesla's work?
a) His innovations are no longer in use.
b) His work is only recognized by a few scientists.
c) His ideas were mostly theoretical and not practical.
d) His contributions are still significant today.

8. Which of the following best summarizes the overall tone of the passage?
a) Admiring and respectful
b) Critical and dismissive
c) Neutral and detached
d) Humorous and light-hearted

 **Activity 1:** In the upcoming activity, you will research one of the listed individuals who have made significant contributions to society and left a lasting legacy. Select a personality, delve into their life story, and document your findings using the provided biography template. This will guide your research and help organize your writing.

1. **Ida B. Wells**
2. **John Steinbeck**
3. **Hedy Lamarr**
4. **Estée Lauder**

Biography Template

SECTION	DESCRIPTION	DETAILS TO RESEARCH and INCLUDE
Introduction	Brief introduction to the person.	• Full name and any famous nicknames. • Birth and death dates (if applicable). • Overview of their significance.
Early Life	Information about the person's early years.	• Date and place of birth. • Family background. • Early education and influences. • Key events or experiences that shaped them.
Major Achievements	Detailed account of the person's key accomplishments.	• Description of their major contributions or achievements. • Impact of their work on their field or the world. • Awards, honors, or recognitions received.
Challenges	Challenges or obstacles they faced in their personal life or career.	• Personal hardships or professional setbacks. • How they overcame these challenges.
Personal Life	Insight into their private life.	• Marital status, family, and notable relationships. • Hobbies or personal interests.
Legacy and Impact	The lasting impact of their work and life.	• How they are remembered today. • Influence on future generations or contemporary society. • Institutions or works named after them.
Conclusion	Summary of their life and why they are significant.	• Recap of their major life events and contributions. • Their place in history or contemporary context.

The Biography of _____   **Author:** _____

Free Supplementary Resource File with Worksheets.

This supplementary resource is aimed to further support the lessons in this book.

Scan the QR Code:

Or visit:
https://natashascripts.com/spelling-writing-and-reading-7th-and-8th-grade-language-arts-curriculum/

Password: SuppResSWR7-8

Skyrocket your 7th Grader's Vocabulary and Spelling Skills with these comprehensive series of workbooks. You will be impressed by your 7th Grader's improvement in word knowledge and usage.

- 36 lessons
- Targets Vocabulary
- Definitions
- Fill-in-the-blanks
- Answer key
- Ideal for Summer

- Intensive Focus
- 16 lessons
- Definitions
- Model Sentences
- Targets Vocabulary and Spelling
- Varied Practice Activities
- Answer key
- Tests
- Test Score Table
- For the classroom
- For homeschooling

- Intensive Focus
- 20 lessons
- Spelling drills in Syllables
- Normal Spelling drills
- Focus on tricky letter positions
- Synonyms
- Sentence writing
- For the classroom
- For homeschooling

6th Grade

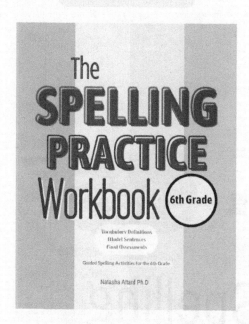

8th Grade

- 20 lessons
- Definitions
- Model Sentences
- Syllable Spelling
- Tricky letter Positioning
- Synonyms Word Search
- Synonyms Activity
- Final Tests
- Answer key
- Ideal as support to Writing Currciulum

- 20 lessons
- Definitions
- Model Sentences
- Syllable Spelling
- Tricky Letter Positioning
- Synonyms Word Search
- Final Tests
- Answer key
- Ideal as support to Writing Curriculum

Available on AMAZON

Answer Key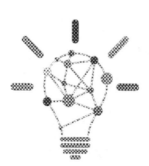

Lesson 2, Activity 1.
1. Word bank 2 has a long "a" sound.
2. Word bank 1 has a short "a" sound.

Lesson 4, Activity 1.

	Short	Long	Silent	Schwa "uh"
D**e**tail		✓		
Equilibrium	✓			
Probl**e**m				✓
Facad**e**			✓	
Extr**e**me		✓		
Sev**e**re		✓		
Epidemic	✓			
Independ**e**nt				✓
Enduranc**e**			✓	
Man**e**uver			✓	
En**e**my				✓
Envision	✓			
It**e**m				✓

Lesson 5, Activity 1.

	L	S		L	S
Invoke		✓	**I**mpede		✓
Implore		✓	Inc**i**te	✓	
Ab**i**de	✓		**I**nviolable		✓
Def**i**ant	✓		**I**mmense		✓
Quagm**i**re	✓		Infur**i**ate	✓	
F**i**lter		✓	Der**i**de	✓	

Lesson 6, Activity 1.

	L	S		L	S
Overdue	✓		R**o**bust	✓	
Occurrence		✓	Prov**o**ke	✓	
Obscure		✓	Er**o**sion	✓	
Obsolete		✓	**O**minous		✓
Alim**o**ny	✓		**O**scillate		✓
Forecl**o**sure	✓		Gr**o**tesque	✓	

Lesson 7, Activity 1.

	L	S		L	S
F**u**ndamental		✓	Rupt**u**re		✓
Unique	✓		Ref**u**se	✓	
Am**u**se	✓		Acc**u**se	✓	
S**u**ccumb		✓	N**u**rture		✓
J**u**dgment		✓	Cons**u**mable	✓	
H**u**mane	✓		Pl**u**mmet		✓

Lesson 8, Activity 1.
1. yielded
2. lie
3. patient
4. grief
5. receipt
6. sovereign
7. surveillance
8. achieve
9. deceive
10. heist
11. counterfeit
12. perceive
13. neighbor
14. ancient
15. efficient
16. reindeer

Lesson 10, Activity 1.

1. The repetition of the 's' and 'str' sounds in the phrase "something strange stirred under the starlit sky" creates a soft, whisper-like sound that adds a mysterious and intriguing mood to the beginning of the story. This use of alliteration, where several words start with the same sound, helps set a calm yet eerie atmosphere.

2. In the story, we find several examples of alliteration, such as "something strange stirred," "stars silently," "tiptoed toward," and "feathered friend." These repeating sounds help make the scenes more vivid. For example, "something strange stirred" adds a sense of mystery, "stars silently" sets a quiet nighttime mood, "tiptoed toward" shows careful movement, and "feathered friend" adds a soft, friendly feel. Each alliteration enhances the imagery, making the story's atmosphere more engaging and lively for the reader.

Lesson 10, Activity 1 (continued).

3. The consonant sounds in "tiny, trembling starling" effectively convey the bird's fragile state. The repeated 't' sound highlights its smallness and vulnerability, adding tension and emphasizing the seriousness of the starling's condition. This use of consonants deepens the emotional impact of the scene.

4. The consonant sounds in the phrase "wrapped in his scarf and rushed home" enhance the sense of quick and decisive action. The repeated 'r' sound in "wrapped," "scarf," and "rushed" rolls off the tongue, mimicking the rapid movement of Hunter as he cares for the starling. This repetition, coupled with the urgent connotation of "rushed," effectively conveys the swift and immediate actions taken by Hunter, emphasizing the urgency and care in his movements.

5. The consonant sounds in "soft rustling" and "wind-swept trees" create auditory imagery that enhances the setting by mimicking the sounds of a quiet, gentle breeze moving through the leaves. The soft 's' sounds in both phrases evoke a sense of calm and serenity, helping the reader imagine a peaceful, natural scene. The 't' sounds add a subtle crispness that suggests the rustle of leaves, adding depth and texture to the visual and auditory landscape of the story.

Lesson 11, Activity 1.

Conflict	1C -2C hard	**Grapple**	G- hard
Govern	G- hard	**Ceremony**	C- soft
Gesture	G- soft	**Cynical**	1C- soft; 2C- hard
Germinate	G- soft	**Compress**	C- hard
Conclude	1C- hard; 2C- hard		

Census	C- soft
Genesis	G- soft
Cilantro	C- soft

Lesson 18, Activity 1.

Refer	Referring	Referred
Prefer	Preferring	Preferred
Begin	Beginning	*
Control	Controlling	Controlled
Commit	Committing	Committed
Admit	Admitting	Admitted
Permit	Permitting	Permitted
Regret	Regretting	Regretted
Equip	Equipping	Equipped
Expel	Expelling	Expelled
Compel	Compelling	Compelled

Lesson 18, Activity 2.

Occur	Occurring	Occurred
Encroach	Encroaching	Encroached
Rebel	Rebelling	Rebelled
Concur	Concurring	Concurred
Handpick	Handpicking	Handpicked
Vanquish	Vanquishing	Vanquished
Perceive	Perceiving	Perceived
Auction	Auctioning	Auctioned
Claim	Claiming	Claimed

Lesson 19, Activity 1.

Cancel	Canceling	Canceled
Control	Controlling	Controlled
Rebel	Rebelling	Rebelled
Label	Labeling	Labeled
Channel	Channeling	Channeled
Travel	Traveling	Traveled
Model	Modeling	Modeled
Unseal	Unsealing	Unsealed
Resell	Reselling	*
Compel	Compelling	Compelled
Signal	Signaling	Signaled
Marshal	Marshaling	Marshaled

Lesson 19, Activity 1 (continued).

Outsell	**Outselling**	*
Extol	**Extolling**	Extolled
Propel	**Propelling**	Propelled
Appeal	**Appealing**	Appealed
Retell	**Retelling**	*
Quarrel	**Quarreling**	Quarreled
Revel	**Reveling**	Reveled
Recall	**Recalling**	Recalled
Repeal	**Repealing**	Repealed
Shovel	**Shoveling**	Shoveled
Repel	**Repelling**	Repelled
Instill	**Instilling**	Instilled
Counsel	**Counseling**	Counseled
Expel	**Expelling**	Expelled
Fuel	**Fueling**	Fueled
Distill	**Distilling**	Distilled
Enthrall	**Enthralling**	Enthralled
Refuel	**Refueling**	Refueled

Lesson 20, Activity 1.

Fathom	Huff
Feign	Puff
Coffee	Scuffle
Enough	Traffic
Tough	Physics
Muffin	Philosophy
Stiff	Photosynthesis
Waffle	
Wharf	
Offering	
Waft	
Forsake	
Laugh	
Trough	

Lesson 21, Activity 2.

Ache, Crave, Wane.

Lesson 21, Activity 3.

A - cre
A - li - en
De - bate
Fa - ble
Sa - li - ent

Lesson 22, Activity 1.

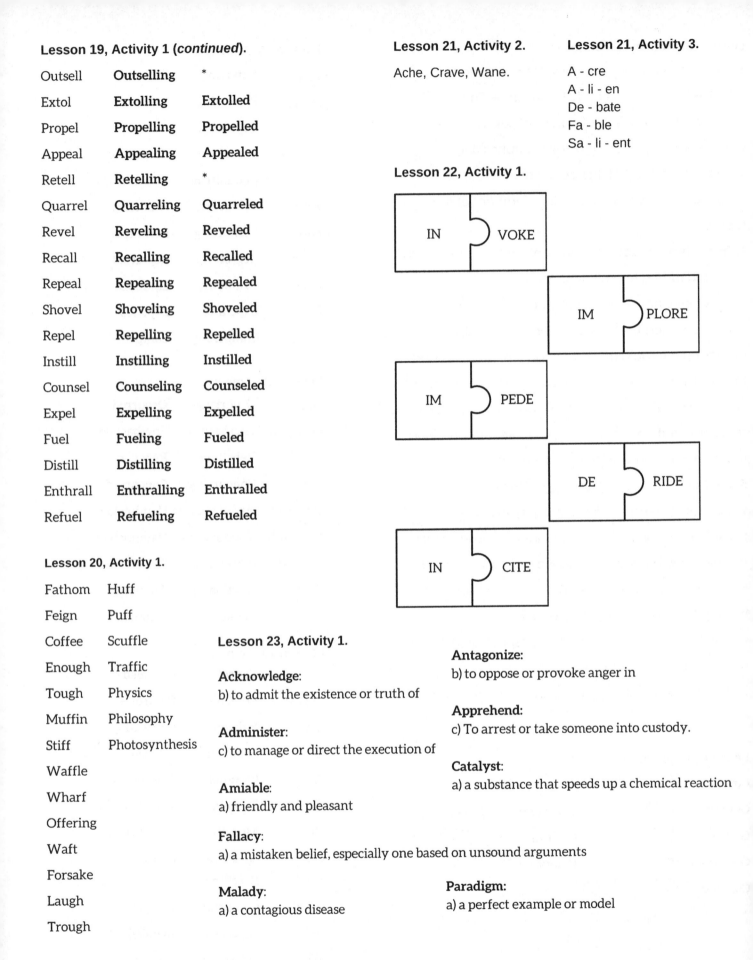

IN VOKE

IM PLORE

IM PEDE

DE RIDE

IN CITE

Lesson 23, Activity 1.

Acknowledge:
b) to admit the existence or truth of

Administer:
c) to manage or direct the execution of

Amiable:
a) friendly and pleasant

Fallacy:
a) a mistaken belief, especially one based on unsound arguments

Malady:
a) a contagious disease

Antagonize:
b) to oppose or provoke anger in

Apprehend:
c) To arrest or take someone into custody.

Catalyst:
a) a substance that speeds up a chemical reaction

Paradigm:
a) a perfect example or model

268

Lesson 23, Activity 2.

1. Salient; 2. Fable; 3. Debate; 4. Acre; 5. Crave;
6. Alien; 7. Ache; 8. Wane.

Lesson 25, Activity 1.

1. I think this sport is extreme because the athlete climbs the toughest mountain peaks in harsh weather, needing incredible physical and mental strength. The dangerous conditions and the balance between pushing limits and respecting nature make it really intense.
2. (i) stamina
3. (ii) mild weather
4. "balance"
5. This story is about an athlete who is known for tackling some of the world's most challenging mountain climbs. He faces harsh weather and tough terrain with incredible physical stamina and mental focus, showing a unique balance between pushing his limits and respecting the power of nature.

Lesson 25, Activity 2.

1. (B) imagine
2. (C) Stories of historical Significance.
3. (C) The spirit of resistance fighters.
4. False
5. False
6. True

Lesson 26, Activity 1.

1. A. endurance; B. maneuver; C. severe; D. extreme.
2. A. item; B. detail; C. equilibrium.
3. A. severe; B. problem; C. extreme.

Lesson 26, Activity 3.

1. B; 2. C; 3. B; 4. C; 5. B.

Lesson 26, Activity 4.

1. deride
2. invoked
3. incite
4. impeded
5. implored
6. implored
7. incite
8. impeded
9. invoked
10. deride

Lesson 26, Activity 5.

1. C) Follow or adhere to
2. B) Boldly resistant or challenging
3. C) A complex, difficult situation.
4. C) A device to remove contaminants.
5. A) Sacred and must not be infringed.
6. B) Extremely large or vast.
7. C) Make very angry.
8. A) Ridicule.

Lesson 27, Activity 1.

1. **Alimony**: Money paid to an ex-husband or ex-wife after a divorce.
2. **Erosion**: The slow wearing away of land or rock by water, wind, or other natural forces.
3. **Foreclosure**: When the bank takes away a house because the owner didn't pay the mortgage.
4. **Grotesque**: Very ugly and strange in a way that doesn't seem normal.
5. **Provoke**: To cause someone to react, often with anger, by saying or doing something.
6. **Robust**: Strong and sturdy, able to handle tough conditions.

Lesson 27, Activity 2.

1. nosedive - plummet
2. edible - consumable
3. care for - nurture
4. critical decision - judgment
5. humane
6. one-of-a-kind - unique

Lesson 27, Activity 3.

1. A) Gave in to pressure of temptation
2. C) Charged with wrongdoing
3. C) Decline
4. C) Basic and necessary
5. C) Burst open
6. B) Entertain

Lesson 28, Activity 1.

1. A. alimony; B. overdue; C. occurrence; D. provoke.
2. A. erosion; B. ominous; C. robust.
3. A. grotesque; B. obscure; C. oscillate.
4. A. foreclosure; B. obsolete.

Lesson 30, Activity 2.

1. Meaning of "**monologue**": A long speech by one person in a play or movie.
2. Meaning of "**monopoly**": When one company is the only one that sells or produces something, blocking others from selling the same thing.
3. Meaning of "**monochrome**": Art or images in only one color or shades of one color, like black and white photos.
4. Meaning of "**monocle**": A single eyeglass kept in position over one eye, used to see things more clearly.
5. Meaning of "**unicycle**": A cycle with only one wheel, which a person rides by balancing carefully.
6. Meaning of "**unison**": When everyone does something together at the same time, like singing or moving together.
7. Meaning of "**bilateral**": Involving two sides or parties, typically referring to agreements or negotiations between two countries or groups.
8. Meaning of "**bilingual**": Able to speak two languages fluently, often resulting in a deeper understanding of different cultures.
9. Meaning of "**dichotomy**": A division or contrast between two things that are presented as opposites or entirely different.
10. Meaning of "**dilemma**": A situation where a difficult choice has to be made between two or more alternatives, especially equally undesirable ones.
11. Meaning of "**triathlon**": A sporting event that includes three different activities: swimming, cycling, and running.
12. Meaning of "**quadrilateral**": A type of shape that has four sides and four angles. Examples include squares, rectangles, and other four-sided figures.
13. Meaning of "**pentagon**": A geometric shape that has five sides and five angles. It can be regular (all sides and angles equal) or irregular.
14. Meaning of "**hexagon**": A shape that has six sides and six angles.
15. Meaning of "**octagonal**": Having eight sides and angles.
16. Meaning of "**decade**": A period of 10 years.

Lesson 31, Activity 2.

Sub: Subway, subtract, submerge.
Inter: International, interact, intercept.
Super: Superstar, supermarket, superhero.
Sur: Surpass, surreal, survive.
Trans: Transport, translate, transform.
Intra: Intramural, intrastate, intravenous.
Exo: Exoskeleton, Exothermic, Exotic.

Lesson 31, Activity 3.

1. Submarine
2. Interactive
3. Superior
4. Surmount
5. Translucent
6. Intravenous
7. Intranet
8. Exoskeleton
9. Exodus
10. Subdue
11. Intercept
12. Superimpose
13. Supersede
14. Transcribing
15. Intracellular
16. Exosphere
17. Subzero
18. Intermingled
19. Surpassed

Lesson 33, Activity 2.

1. folded
2. seen
3. unseen
4. untied
5. veil
6. leashed
7. unfolded
8. tied
9. unveil
10. unleashed

Lesson 33, Activity 4.

1. unbiased
2. sustainable
3. finished
4. unaware
5. unsustainable
6. unfounded
7. (well-)founded
8. common
9. uncommon
10. undeniable
11. unyielding
12. unfinished
13. biased
14. deniable
15. yielding

Lesson 34, Activity 2.

1. polite
2. permeable
3. impolite
4. possible
5. mobile
6. imperfect
7. measurable
8. practical
9. partial
10. immutable
11. immobile
12. perfect
13. mutable
14. mortal
15. immature
16. immeasurable
17. immortal
18. mature
19. impractical
20. impartial
21. impermeable
22. impossible

Lesson 34, Activity 4.

1. irrecoverable
2. irreproachable   6. irrelevant
3. irresponsible   7. irrational
4. irregular   8. irrefutable
5. irreversible   9. irresolvable

Lesson 34, Activity 6.

1. illogical   5. illiterate
2. illuminous   6. illegible
3. illegitimate   7. illegal
4. illiberal

Lesson 34, Activity 8.

1. inactive   11. flexible
2. active   12. inflexible
3. incorrect   13. intolerant
4. correct   14. tolerant
5. direct   15. visible
6. indirect   17. invisible
7. dependent   18. invalidate
8. independent   19. injustice
9. indecent   20. justice
10. decent   21. ability
     22. inability

Lesson 34, Activity 10.

1. Inclusion - "industrious" means "showing diligent work within tasks."

2. Negation - "independent" means "not dependent."

3. Inclusion - "inhabit" means "to dwell or live within a place."

4. Direction - "inject" means "to force a liquid into something."

5. Negation - "invalidate" means "to make not valid."

6. Negation - "injustice" means "not just or fair."

7. Negation - "inflexible" means "not flexible."

8. Addition - "inflate" means "to fill with air or gas."

9. Direction - "inspect" means "to look closely into something."

Lesson 35 Activity 1.

1. Disadvantage: A condition or situation that makes it more difficult to succeed.
2. Disaggregate: To separate into parts.
3. Disapprove: To have a negative opinion of.
4. Disarmament: The reduction or elimination of weapons.
5. Disarray: A state of disorder.
6. Disassemble: To take apart.
7. Discomfort: A state of slight pain or unease.
8. Disconcert: To unsettle or confuse.
9. Discontent: A state of dissatisfaction.
10. Discontinue: To stop or end.
11. Discrepancy: A difference or inconsistency.
12. Disenfranchise: To deprive of the right to vote.
13. Dishearten: To cause a loss of hope or confidence.
14. Disinherit: To prevent someone from receiving an inheritance.

Lesson 35 Activity 2.

1. mislead   11. misspell
2. misusing   12. miscalculated
3. misuse   13. misinterpreted
4. misdirected   14. misquoted
5. misinterpret   15. misfire
6. misunderstand   16. misquote
7. mistreat   17. mismanaged
8. misspring   18. misapply
9. misbehave   19. misplace
10. miscalculate   20. misdiagnosed

Lesson 35 Activity 4.

1. antidote   9. noncompetitive
2. nonexistent   10. nonconformist
3. antagonist   11. antibody
4. nonfiction   12. antifungal
5. anticorrosive   13. nonstop
6. nontoxic   14. nonviolent
7. antioxidant   15. nonnegotiable
8. antithesis   16. nonessential

Lesson 37 Activity 1.

1. playful   9. careful   17. grateful
2. beautiful   10. plentiful   18. eventful
3. wonderful   11. merciful   19. deceitful
4. joyful   12. resourceful   20. remorseful
5. peaceful   13. spiteful   21. sorrowful
6. thoughtful   14. vengeful   22. mournful
7. graceful   15. cheerful
8. helpful   16. respectful

Lesson 38 Activity 1.

1. hopeless
2. careless
3. endless
4. homeless
5. fearless
6. priceless
7. thoughtless
8. tireless
9. reckless
10. speechless
11. worthless
12. fruitless
13. aimless
14. motionless
15. sleepless

Lesson 39 Activity 1.

enjoyable possible inevitable
likeable visible viable
appealable credible navigable
distillable accessible portable
repealable reversible applicable
draftable collapsible capable
audible sensible tolerable
flexible durable

Lesson 39 Activity 2.

1. comprehensible
2. suspendible
3. defensible
4. apprehensible
5. impoundable
6. comprehensible
7. impoundable
8. suspendible
9. apprehensible
10. defensible

Lesson 40 Activity 2.

1. b) Able to be heard
2. d) Theater
3. a) A decision
4. b) A law
5. b) A crossing
6. c) Sells abroad
7. a) Hold up
8. a) A collection of works
9. b) A handwritten document
10. a) Proof

Lesson 40 Activity 4.

1. chronicle
2. antibiotics
3. autobiography
4. hydroelectric
5. asteroid
6. microchip
7. synchronized
8. dialogue
9. geology
10. graphics
11. hydration
12. astronaut
13. apology

Lesson 41 Activity 1.

1. c)
2. a)
3. d)
4. c)
5. d)
6. b)
7. c)
8. a)
9. d)
10. c)

Lesson 42 Activity 1.

Defiant - Rebellious
Quagmire - Chaos
Deride - Mock
Infuriate - Enrage
Abide - Comply
Inviolable - Sacred

Lesson 42 Activity 2.
PAIR 1
A. Defiant **B.** Rebellious
A. Follow **B.** Adhere

PAIR 2
A. Deride **B.** Mock
A. Infuriate **B.** Enrage

Lesson 42 Activity 3.

Obscure - Hidden or Cryptic
Obsolete - Antiquated or Outdated
Occurrence - Event or Incident
Ominous - Foreboding or Threatening
Oscillate - Swing or Fluctuate
Overdue - Late or Delayed

Lesson 42 Activity 4.

1. Obsolete
2. Obscure
3. Ominous
4. Overdue
5. Quagmire
6. Infuriated
7. Deride
8. Rebellious, Defiant

Lesson 43 Activity 2.

1. Despite the **intensity** of the desert heat, the explorers continued their journey.
Explanation: "Intensity" conveys the extreme degree of heat.
"Harsh": Can be used; it implies severity but is less specific about the degree.
"Severe": Could fit; it indicates seriousness but is more general and might not capture the extremeness as well as "intensity."

2. The student's **endurance** during the marathon was impressive, showing both physical and mental strength.
Explanation: "Endurance" refers to the ability to withstand hardship over time.
"Stamina": Could be used; it focuses more on physical staying power.
"Perseverance": Also suitable; it emphasizes persistence and determination, which includes mental strength.

3. The scientist served as a **catalyst** for the project, inspiring his team to think creatively.
Explanation: "Catalyst" refers to something that causes change or inspires action.
"Stimulus": Appropriate; it means something that encourages activity but may not suggest the same transformative impact as "catalyst."
"Trigger": Could fit; it implies something that initiates a process but may not capture the broader inspirational impact.

4. His decision to drop out of school was based on a common **fallacy**, that you don't need education to succeed.
Explanation: "Fallacy" refers to a mistaken belief or misconception.
"Misconception": Suitable; it also means a wrong belief but may not emphasize incorrect reasoning as strongly as "fallacy."
"Error": Less fitting; it suggests a mistake but doesn't necessarily imply a false belief.

5. The small non-profit organization operated **independently**, relying on donations and volunteer work.
Explanation: "Independently" means functioning without reliance on others.
"Self-reliantly": Could be used; it also means relying on oneself but might feel redundant with "operated."
"Autonomously": Suitable; it emphasizes self-governance and freedom from external control.

6. To **navigate** through the dense forest, they had to follow the marked trails carefully.
Explanation: "Navigate" means finding one's way through a difficult path or environment.
"Maneuver": Could be used; it implies skillful movement but is less specific about finding a path.
"Move": Less fitting; it is too general and doesn't convey the idea of carefully finding a way through.

7. The manager tried not to **antagonize** the employees, understanding that a happy workforce is more productive.
Explanation: "Antagonize" means to provoke or irritate someone.
"Provoke": Could be used; it means to incite but may suggest a more deliberate action.
"Irritate": Suitable; it means to annoy but might not capture the idea of creating conflict as well as "antagonize."

8. She didn't fully **appreciate** the significance of the gesture until much later.
Explanation: "Appreciate" means to recognize the full worth or significance of something.
"Value": Could be used; it means to regard something as important but may not capture the idea of understanding.
"Recognize": Suitable; it means to be aware of something but might not imply the depth of understanding as "appreciate."

9. The outbreak of the **malady** spread quickly, affecting a large part of the population.
Explanation: "Malady" refers to a disease or illness.
"Illness": Suitable; it also means disease but might not carry the same formal tone.
"Disease": Appropriate; it means an illness but might not capture the seriousness as well as "malady."

Lesson 44 Activity 1.

1. **Correct**: They **dismissed** his suggestion without even considering its potential benefits.
Explanation: "Dismissed" is the best fit because it means to disregard or ignore something, often in a more formal or definitive way. This accurately describes the action of not considering the suggestion's potential benefits. "Dismissed" conveys a sense of a deliberate decision to reject or ignore the suggestion, which aligns with the context of not considering its potential benefits. "Disregarded" could also fit but is less suitable here because it often implies a more casual or less formal act of ignoring. While "disregarded" means to pay no attention to something, it doesn't carry the same weight of a formal or intentional decision as "dismissed" does.

2. **Correct**: The child was so **dependent** on his parents that he couldn't make decisions on his own.
Explanation: "Dependent" is the best fit because it means relying on someone else for support or help, which accurately describes the child's relationship with his parents. "Dependent" is a commonly used term in contexts where someone relies on another for significant support or guidance, fitting well with the idea of a child being unable to make decisions independently. "Reliant" could also fit but is less suitable here because it generally implies a less absolute form of dependency. While "reliant" does mean depending on someone, it often suggests a degree of self-sufficiency and a more balanced form of reliance. For instance, a person might be reliant on their car for transportation but is not helpless without it.

3. **Correct**: After only a few hours of hiking, she felt extreme **fatigue** and needed to rest.
Explanation: "Fatigue" is the best fit because it specifically refers to tiredness and exhaustion. "Weakness" could fit, but it is more general and does not capture the sense of tiredness as precisely as "fatigue."

4. **Correct**: The lack of funding was a major **hindrance** to the project's progress.
Explanation: "Hindrance" is the best fit because it means something that delays or obstructs progress, which accurately describes how the lack of funding affects the project. "Hindrance" is a commonly used term in contexts where an element is impeding progress or making it difficult to proceed, fitting well with the idea of funding issues obstructing the project's progress. "Obstacle" could also fit but is less suitable here because "obstacle" often implies a more tangible or substantial barrier. While "obstacle" means something that obstructs or impedes, it tends to be used in contexts where the barrier is more concrete or significant. In contrast, "hindrance" suggests a general impediment that can be either a minor or major issue, making it more flexible for various contexts.

5. **Correct**: The **severe** weather caused the city to shut down all services.
Explanation: "Severe" is the best fit because it implies extreme weather conditions that could justify shutting down services. "Gentle" and "mild" would not make sense as they imply calm weather.

6. **Correct**: The **truth** about the incident finally came to light, clearing up many misunderstandings.
Explanation: "Truth" is the best fit because it directly opposes "fallacy," meaning an incorrect belief or misconception. The sentence describes a situation where the actual facts or reality of the incident are revealed, which clears up misunderstandings. "Truth" conveys the idea of correctness and accuracy in a broader and more philosophical sense, fitting well with the context of revealing the true nature of the incident. "Fact" could also fit but is less suitable here because it often refers to a specific piece of information rather than the broader concept of correctness and accuracy. While "fact" means a piece of information that is objectively true, "truth" encompasses a more comprehensive understanding of reality and correctness, which aligns better with the context of clearing up misunderstandings about an incident.

7. **Correct**: Her sense of **wellness** improved significantly after she started meditating daily.
Explanation: "Wellness" is the best fit because it captures a broader sense of overall well-being. "Health" could also fit but focuses more on physical condition, whereas "wellness" includes mental and emotional well-being.

8. **Correct**: Winning the scholarship was a **blessing**, allowing her to attend college without financial worries.
Explanation: "Blessing" is the best fit because it implies a positive and fortunate event. "Success" is not a good fit as "winning the scholarship" already implies success, and it does not convey the intended meaning of a "fortunate event."

9. **Correct**: She was **dependent** on her tutor for help with every assignment.
Explanation: "Dependent" is the best fit because it means relying on someone else for support or help. It accurately describes her reliance on her tutor. "Reliant" could also fit but is less suitable because "dependent" is more commonly used in this context to describe a more significant and continuous need for assistance.

10. **Correct**: He **stumbled** over his words during the presentation, losing the audience's attention.
Explanation: "Stumbled" is the best fit because it means to trip or falter in speech, which fits the context of losing the audience's

attention. "Hesitated" would not be correct because "hesitated over" is not a commonly used phrase and does not convey the continuous difficulty implied by "stumbled." "Hesitated" implies a momentary pause rather than a continuous difficulty.

11. **Correct**: She **hesitated** before answering the question, unsure of her response.
Explanation: "Hesitated" is the best fit because it means pausing before acting or speaking. "Stumbled" could fit, but it implies making mistakes, which is not the intended meaning here.

12. **Correct**: The committee **dismissed** her concerns as irrelevant to the discussion.
Explanation: "Dismissed" is the best fit because it means to disregard or ignore. "Disregarded" could also fit, but "dismissed" is more commonly used in formal contexts.

13. **Correct**: The gentle music helped to **soothe** the anxious crowd.
Explanation: "Soothe" is the best fit because it means to calm or relieve, which aligns with the effect of gentle music. "Pacify" could also fit because it means to bring peace or calm, but "soothe" is more commonly used in the context of music. "Pacify" often implies a more active intervention to bring about peace or calmness, such as in conflict resolution, while "soothe" is typically used for more passive, gentle actions like playing calming music.

14. **Correct**: The cat's **gentle** purring was very soothing to the children.
Explanation: "Gentle" is the best fit because it directly opposes "severe," implying a soft and calming sound, which fits the context of soothing purring. "Mild" could also fit, but "gentle" is more commonly used to describe the soft and comforting nature of purring. "Mild" is less suitable here because it usually describes something that lacks intensity or strength, and is more often used with conditions like "mild weather" or "mild flavor," where it contrasts with something harsh or strong. In contrast, "gentle" conveys a sense of tenderness and care, making it a more appropriate choice for describing purring.

15. **Correct**: The new marketing strategy was a huge **success**, increasing sales dramatically.
Explanation: "Success" is the best fit because it directly opposes "catastrophe," implying a positive outcome that aligns perfectly with the context of increased sales. While "blessing" can imply a fortunate event, it often carries a connotation of unexpected good fortune or a stroke of luck. In the context of a marketing strategy, "success" is more appropriate because it indicates the intended and planned positive result of the strategy.

16. **Correct**: Regular exercise and a balanced diet contribute greatly to good **health**.
Explanation: "Health" is the best fit because it directly opposes "malady," which means illness or disease, implying a good physical condition. "Wellness" could also fit but is less suitable here because "wellness" often refers to a broader concept that includes not just physical health, but also mental and emotional well-being. In this context, the sentence focuses specifically on the physical benefits of regular exercise and a balanced diet, making "health" the more precise and appropriate choice.

17. **Correct**: The **truth** that the Earth orbits the Sun is well-established in science.
Explanation: "Truth" is the best fit because it directly opposes "fallacy," which means a false belief or misconception. "Fact" could also fit but is less suitable here because "truth" emphasizes the correctness and accuracy of the belief in a broader philosophical sense.

18. **Correct**: The strict regulations acted as an **obstacle** to the company's expansion plans.
Explanation: "Obstacle" is the best fit because it directly opposes "catalyst," which means something that accelerates a process. "Obstacle" implies something that hinders or prevents progress, fitting the context of strict regulations impeding expansion plans. The sentence offers the article "an," which indicates that the word following it must begin with a vowel sound. This makes "hindrance" a lesser fit grammatically. Additionally, "hindrance" often refers to a minor or less significant impediment, whereas "obstacle" more strongly conveys the idea of a significant barrier, aligning better with the context of substantial regulations affecting expansion plans.

19. **Correct**: The diplomat's calming words were able to **soothe** the angry protesters.
Explanation: "Soothe" is the best fit because it directly opposes "antagonize," which means to provoke or irritate. "Soothe" means to calm or relieve, aligning with the context of calming words. "Pacify" could also fit but is less suitable here because "soothe" is more commonly used for gentle calming actions, especially in the context of words or actions that bring about peace or relief. "Pacify" often implies a more active and sometimes forceful intervention to bring about peace or calmness, such as in conflict resolution or dealing with an unruly crowd. For example, a government might pacify a rebellion, which indicates a more active and forceful approach, whereas "soothe" implies a more gentle and passive calming effect, suitable for describing the effect of calming words.

20. **Correct**: His **weakness** became apparent when he couldn't lift the weights he used to handle with ease.
Explanation: "Weakness" is the best fit because it implies a lack of strength, fitting the context of being unable to lift weights. "Fatigue" could also fit but is less suitable as it specifically refers to tiredness, while "weakness" captures the general sense of diminished strength.

275

Lesson 47 Activity 2.

Coarse / Course
1. She signed up for a short **course** in digital marketing.
2. The towels were made from a very **coarse** material.

Affect / Effect
3. The **effect** of the new policy on employee morale was noticeable immediately.
4. The new manager's leadership style will **affect** the team's performance.

Capital / Capitol
5. The startup is seeking additional **capital** to fund its expansion.
6. The protest took place outside the state **capitol** building.

Accept / Except
7. He decided to **accept** the job offer after much consideration.
8. All students, **except** John, must submit their essays by Friday.

Complement / Compliment
9. He received a **compliment** on his new haircut.
10. The chef used fresh herbs to **complement** the flavors in the dish.

Principle / Principal
11. The scientist refused to compromise his **principle** during the debate.
12. The **principal** of the school is retiring at the end of the year.

Stationary / Stationery
13. She wrote her thank-you notes on personalized **stationery**.
14. The artwork should remain **stationary** to avoid damage.

Lesson 47 Activity 4.

Desert / Dessert
1. Many animals have adapted to survive in the harsh **desert** conditions.
2. Chocolate cake is her favorite **dessert** after dinner.

Elicit / Illicit
3. The speaker's question was meant to **elicit** a reaction from the audience.
4. They were arrested for trading **illicit** substances.

Ensure / Insure
5. He decided to **insure** his car against theft.
6. Please double-check the figures to **ensure** accuracy in the report.

Further / Farther
7. Is the parking lot much **farther** from here?
8. This study aims to **further** our understanding of climate change.

Precede / Proceed
9. Please **proceed** to the next chapter after completing the exercises.
10. The opening remarks will **precede** the award ceremony.

Device / Devise
11. You can track your daily steps with this small wearable **device**.
12. We need to **devise** a strategy to improve our sales numbers.

Lesson 47 Activity 5.

1. a) devise
2. b) affect
3. b) precede
4. a) complemented
5. b) further
6. a) principle
7. a) except
8. a) ensure
9. b) coarse
10. b) elicit
11. b) illicit
12. b) dessert
13. a) stationary

Lesson 49: Reading Comprehension 1 (Narrative Text)

1. c) Exhilarated - The passage describes Noah's excitement and awe upon finding the map.
2. b) Old and worn-out.
3. b) It was less likely to attract attention - The passage states the boat was chosen for its inconspicuousness.
4. c) Adverse weather conditions - The passage describes the vicious North Sea and the perils faced.
5. c) They were suspicious and unwelcoming - The passage notes the residents' hostility towards Noah and the skipper.
6. b) Highlight the dangers and challenges of the quest - The description emphasizes the difficulty and risks involved.
7. c) Beautiful - "Exquisite" is used to describe the valuable and attractive nature of the treasure.
8. a) He was overwhelmed by the sheer quantity of gold and jewels - The passage describes the treasure as beyond their wildest dreams.
9. b) Transporting the treasure out of the cavern - The next challenge mentioned is transporting the treasure.
10. d) It involves a quest with significant challenges and a valuable reward - The passage follows the adventure narrative structure with a clear quest and challenges.

Lesson 50: Reading Comprehension 2 (Descriptive Text)

1. a) To describe the scenic beauty and attractions of the Grand Canyon - The passage focuses on the visual splendor and various activities available at the Grand Canyon.
2. c) Enormous - The word "immense" in the context of describing the Grand Canyon refers to its vast size.
3. d) Caused by different times of day and mineral content - The passage explains that the colors change due to the varying mineral content in the rock layers and the angle of the sunlight.
4. b) Hikers on this trail should be prepared for both beautiful scenery and a physically demanding journey. The passage emphasizes both the visual appeal and the difficulty of the hike, implying that the experience is intended to be both rewarding and physically challenging.
5. b) It is a feature that adds to the adventure and scenic beauty of the canyon - The Colorado River provides opportunities for thrilling rafting trips and adds to the scenic beauty.
6. a) It offers a variety of activities that cater to different interests - The passage mentions various activities like hiking and rafting, indicating its broad appeal.
7. a) Flows gently and peacefully.
8. d) They reveal the Earth's geological history - The layers of rock in the Grand Canyon tell a story of millions of years of geological history.

Lesson 51: Reading Comprehension 3 (Expository Text)

1. b) To explain how to build a simple electric circuit - The passage is a step-by-step guide on building a basic electric circuit.
2. d) Basic - "Fundamental" in this context means basic or essential.
3. c) Preparing the wires - The first step described is to strip the insulation from the wires.
4. a) To secure the wire connections - Electrical tape is used to hold the wire connections in place.
5. a) Recheck all the connections to ensure they are secure - The passage advises checking connections if the bulb does not light up.
6. c) It is the power source - The battery provides the electricity needed for the circuit.
7. b) Tight - "Secure" in this context means ensuring the connections are tight and stable.
8. d) They ensure that the electricity flows properly and the circuit functions correctly.

Lesson 52: Reading Comprehension 4 (Persuasive Text)

1. d) To explain the benefits of a balanced diet.
2. a) Essential.
3. c) Their rich content of vitamins and antioxidants helps enhance immune defense - The essay highlights that fruits and vegetables contain vitamins and antioxidants that are vital for boosting the immune system and protecting the body against infections.
4. b) They aid in muscle maintenance - The essay highlights whole grains and proteins as providing energy and supporting muscle growth and repair.
5. b) Eating nutrient-dense foods can improve mood and reduce the risk of depression and anxiety - The essay discusses the positive connection between a balanced diet and mental health.

Lesson 52: Reading Comprehension 4 (continued)

6. d) They should be avoided for better health - They are linked to obesity, diabetes, and heart disease.
7. a) They enhance mental acuity and support neurological health - The essay highlights that Omega-3 fatty acids support brain health and cognitive function.
8. c) A diet rich in various nutrients is vital for maintaining good health and preventing deficiencies - The conclusion emphasizes the overall benefits of maintaining a balanced diet for health and happiness.

Lesson 53: Reading Comprehension 5 (Report)

1. c) Candy consumption patterns among teenagers in Springfield
2. b) Most teenagers consume candy multiple times throughout the week.
3. a) Self-reported surveys
4. c) 300 grams
5. d) Higher risks of obesity and dental problems.
6. a) The Chart

Lesson 54: Reading Comprehension 6 (Journal Entries)

1. c) Captivating
2. a) To observe and appreciate the natural environment
3. b) "My team didn't win, but we had a lot of fun and learned the value of teamwork and sportsmanship."
4. b) They learned about teamwork and sportsmanship despite not winning - The entry emphasizes the lessons learned and fun had, regardless of winning.
5. d) The writer struggled initially - The entry notes the challenge and eventual reward of succeeding in coding.
6. d) Feeling happy and sad at the same time - "Bittersweet" is used to describe mixed emotions.
7. c) The campfire gathering
8. a) Appreciative

Lesson 54: Reading Comprehension 7 (Legal Letter)

1. a) To protect the client's exclusive rights and investment in their trademark - The letter states that the unauthorized use of the trademark leads to confusion among consumers and dilutes the brand, directly implying the need to protect the client's exclusive rights and investment.
2. d) d) It undermines the uniqueness of their brand in the market - The letter mentions that the infringement has led to confusion among consumers and diluted the distinctive quality of the client's brand, effectively undermining its uniqueness in the market.
3. c) Legal measures will be taken to prevent future misuse. - The letter explicitly warns that if the infringing activities do not cease, the client is prepared to take all necessary legal actions to protect its rights, including seeking an injunction and pursuing claims for damages, indicating steps to prevent future misuse.
4. c) Ceasing the disputed use of the trademark - The letter includes a formal demand that GlobalTech immediately cease and desist from any and all use of the trademark
5. b) b) The inclusion of a specific legal statute as a foundational argument - The letter cites the Lanham Act, specifically Section 32(1).
6. d) It minimizes the risk of misinterpretation and potential legal loopholes - The use of precise language in the letter minimizes risks of misinterpretation.

Lesson 55: Reading Comprehension 8
(Dialogue)

1. b) Due to the influence of his peers - Jayden mentions joining activities because his friends did, indicating peer influence as a primary motivator.
2. c) "The homework load has doubled since last year, and I barely have time for anything else."
3. a) He finds the increased academic workload unmanageable.
4. a) He finds the increased academic workload unmanageable.
5. d) "Maybe I should give more thought to what I really enjoy studying."
6. b) He views it as a critical and potentially overwhelming decision.
7. c) Through mutual support and sharing coping strategies - Both Jayden and William agree that talking helps.

Lesson 56: Reading Comprehension 9
(Newspaper Opinion Article)

1. d) To present both sides of the debate over school uniforms - The article discusses both the pros and cons of school uniforms, providing a balanced view of the issue.
2. a) "Uniforms seem to foster a sense of seriousness and purpose, leading to fewer disruptions and more focus on academics." - This sentence uses more formal language such as "foster," "seriousness" and "purpose," and uses the passive construction ("leading to"). It also uses an impersonal tone.
3. a) Neutral and balanced - The article maintains a neutral tone, presenting both sides of the argument without showing strong bias.
4. b) Make the school environment fair and equal for all students.
5. c) The author sees both benefits and drawbacks to school uniforms - The author discusses both the positive and negative aspects of school uniforms, indicating a balanced perspective.

Lesson 57: Reading Comprehension 10
(Biography)

1. b) Alternating current systems
2. a) Transformed
3. c) Wireless communication - Tesla envisioned a world where information could be transmitted without wires.
4. b) They were never proven - The passage states that Tesla's claims were never substantiated.
5. d) He faced economic hardships - Tesla faced financial difficulties and lived in obscurity in his later years.
6. c) He was not as famous as some of his contemporaries - The passage suggests that Tesla did not achieve the same level of fame during his lifetime.
7. d) His contributions are still significant today - The passage notes that Tesla's innovations continue to impact our daily lives.
8. a) Admiring and respectful - The overall tone of the passage is one of admiration and respect for Tesla's contributions.

Made in the USA
Coppell, TX
20 September 2024

37499962R10155